CANADIANS AT WAR

BATTLE CRIES
IN THE WILDERNESS

THE STRUGGLE FOR NORTH AMERICA
IN THE SEVEN YEARS' WAR

Colonel Bernd Horn

DUNDURN
TORONTO

Project Editor: Michael Carroll
Editor: Cheryl Hawley
Design: Jesse Hooper
Printer: Webcom

Library and Archives Canada Cataloguing in Publication

Horn, Bernd, 1959-
    Battle cries in the wilderness : the struggle for North America in the Seven Years' War / written by Bernd Horn.

Includes bibliographical references and index.
Issued also in electronic formats.
ISBN 978-1-55488-919-8

    1. Canada--History--Seven Years' War, 1755-1763--Juvenile literature.
I. Title.

FC384.H67 2011   j971.01'88   C2011-901912-4

1   2   3   4   5   15   14   13   12   11

We acknowledge the support of the **Canada Council for the Arts** and the **Ontario Arts Council** for our publishing program. We also acknowledge the financial support of the **Government of Canada** through the **Canada Book Fund** and **Livres Canada Books**, and the **Government of Ontario** through the **Ontario Book Publishing Tax Credit** and the **Ontario Media Development Corporation**.

Care has been taken to trace the ownership of copyright material used in this book. The author and the publisher welcome any information enabling them to rectify any references or credits in subsequent editions.

J. Kirk Howard, President

Printed and bound in Canada.
www.dundurn.com

Dundurn	Gazelle Book Services Limited	Dundurn
3 Church Street, Suite 500	White Cross Mills	2250 Military Road
Toronto, Ontario, Canada	High Town, Lancaster, England	Tonawanda, NY
M5E 1M2	LA1 4XS	U.S.A. 14150

CONTENTS

ACKNOWLEDGEMENTS 9

INTRODUCTION 11

CHAPTER 1 – ADAPT OR DIE 25

CHAPTER 2 – THE CANADIAN WAY OF WAR 43

CHAPTER 3 – THE ANGLO-AMERICANS STRIKE BACK 63

CHAPTER 4 – A DEADLY GAME OF CAT AND MOUSE 83

CHAPTER 5 – THE BEGINNING OF THE END 109

EPILOGUE 121

SELECTED READINGS 135

INDEX 139

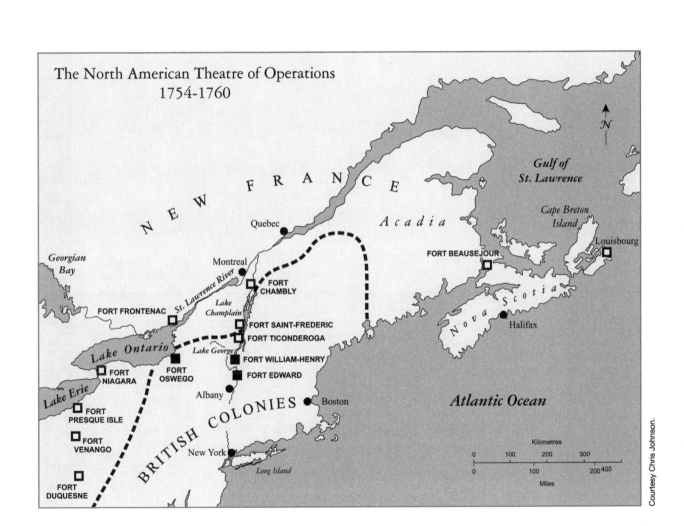

The North American Theatre of Operations 1754-1760

NEW FRANCE

Georgian Bay

Gulf of St. Lawrence

Cape Breton Island

Louisbourg

Quebec

Acadia

FORT BEAUSEJOUR

Montreal

FORT FRONTENAC

St. Lawrence River

Lake Champlain

FORT CHAMBLY

FORT SAINT-FREDERIC

FORT TICONDEROGA

Nova Scotia

Halifax

Lake Ontario

Lake George

FORT OSWEGO

FORT WILLIAM-HENRY

FORT NIAGARA

FORT EDWARD

Lake Erie

Albany

Boston

Atlantic Ocean

FORT PRESQUE ISLE

BRITISH COLONIES

FORT VENANGO

New York

Long Island

FORT DUQUESNE

N

Kilometres

0   100   200   300

0   100   200 400

Miles

ACKNOWLEDGEMENTS

As always in a project such as this, there are many people behind the scenes who have helped in a number of important ways. As such, I wish to acknowledge those who have provided their time, expertise, guidance, and assistance in helping me finish this book.

Initially, I would like to thank Ted Zuber for his continuing friendship and outstanding artwork, as well as Chris Johnson for his detailed map work. I would also be remiss if I did not thank Suzanne Surgeson for her assistance in accessing Parks Canada graphics, and Denise Kerr for her expert editorial support. I must also thank Paramount Press, as well as Robert Flacke Sr., and the Fort William Henry Corporation, who made possible the use of a number of the graphics that are used in the book. In addition, I must also highlight the incredible work of the Dundurn editorial and design team, specifically the project editor, Michael Carroll, and editor Cheryl Hawley, who turned a raw manuscript into the polished product that you hold in your hands. Finally, as always, I wish to thank Kim for her continuing tolerance and patience of my never-ending projects and historical pursuits.

INTRODUCTION

The loud chops echoed through the northern New York forest like thunder-claps. The soldiers, stripped down to their breeches, joked as they wielded their heavy axes to cut down trees for firewood to cook food and to heat the drafty barracks they lived in. Even though it was a cool morning, they already had a film of sweat on their bodies.

Off to the side, a few soldiers stood idly leaning against trees. Although they were supposed to be sentries guarding the wood-cutters, most considered the job a chance to escape the monotony of fort life. None of them thought it was dangerous. After all, Fort William Henry, the northernmost English post in the Lake Champlain Valley was only 800 metres away. What danger could there be with over 500 soldiers and militiamen so close by?

As the soldiers chopped away at the trees, the woods filled with the sound of metal striking wood. Nate Johnson felt the strong vibration in his hands each time the axe head bit into the tree trunk, the collision of steel and wood creating an explosion of energy that travelled up the thick axe handle. After a surge of steady strokes, Nate paused and expelled some air. He lowered his heavy axe to the ground and took a breather. He leaned the axe against the tree

Courtesy Fort William Henry Corporation.

British Grenadier — 48th Regiment of Foot.

and then sat down with his back against the trunk. As he gazed at the others, he saw one of the sentries freeze suddenly, his face caught in a mix of horror and disbelief. For a moment, Nate thought he was dreaming. Sticking out of the back of his skull was a tomahawk. The scene took only seconds to unfold, but it seemed frozen in time. Nate watched as the mortally wounded soldier crumpled to the ground in a lifeless heap without making a sound.

Nate stared, not fully understanding what had just happened. Then a series of shots rang out in quick succession, jolting him from his trance. Everywhere it seemed the British soldiers were falling to the ground, struck down by one or more heavy lead musket balls. Then he heard the dreaded Native war cry — a shrill piercing scream that meant a Native war party was rushing in for the kill. The British soldiers who survived the initial volley of well-aimed shots dropped their axes and rushed for their muskets. Some just froze in place, overwhelmed with fear.

KEY FACTS

The Seven Years' War

The Seven Years' War was arguably one of the first global conflicts. It was fought in Europe, North America, and India, with maritime operations reaching out over the Atlantic and Indian Oceans, as well as the Mediterranean and Caribbean Seas. The war started when Austria, France, Russia, Sweden, and Saxony, deeply concerned over Prussia's growing strength and territorial expansion under Frederick the Great, formed a coalition designed to defeat Prussia. England, which was already in a war with France, formed an alliance with Prussia.

In North America, the conflict (often termed the French and Indian War) actually began two years earlier, in the late spring of 1754. The growing competition for the rich lands of the Ohio Valley were the reason for the latest round of conflict between the French and English colonies. Robert Dinwiddie, the governor of Virginia, concerned with the news that the French and Canadians were solidifying their claim to the Ohio by constructing a series of forts, sent Lieutenant-Colonel George Washington and a detachment of militia to build a fort of their own on the forks of the Ohio River. A confrontation soon followed. Washington and his party were defeated by the French at Great Meadows (Fort Necessity) and pushed back over the Allegheny Mountains. A second attempt by Major-General Braddock was made the following summer, but his force was ambushed near Fort Duquesne and virtually annihilated.

North America eventually became part of the greater conflict. French victories and English setbacks in the early years of the war were reversed by 1758, due to the British decision to focus their strategy and resources on the wilderness campaign. A virtual naval blockade, together with the addition of more than 20,000 British regulars, turned things around. The capture of the Fortress of Louisbourg and Fort Frontenac, in 1758, forced the French to adopt a defensive posture centred around Quebec City and Montreal. The deteriorating French condition also resulted in the defection of a large number of their Native allies. In 1759, the British began to roll up the remaining French forts on the frontier. One army captured Fort Niagara, and another marched up the Lake Champlain/ Richelieu River corridor, while a third invaded Quebec City. The siege ended in September 1759, with the British victory on the Plains of Abraham. The remnants of the French Army and their Canadian militia and remaining Native allies withdrew to Montreal in hopes of recapturing Quebec City in the spring.

Although almost successful, as a result of their victory in the Battle at Sainte-Foy and subsequent siege of Quebec in April 1760, the appearance of the Royal Navy forced the French to return to Montreal, where they later surrendered on September 8, 1760. The war was formally ended in 1763 by the Treaty of Paris, which gave almost all of New France to the British.

As the attackers swarmed in with tomahawks and knives, Nate scrambled for cover, ducking under some low spruce shrubs. He watched in horror as the tragedy unfolded before him. The Natives, dressed in loin cloths and breeches, their torsos and faces painted in hideous colour schemes, suddenly burst from the surrounding forest. Some quickly rushed up to the fallen soldiers and scalped them. Anyone who resisted was struck with a tomahawk or dealt a deadly blow with a knife. The attackers were efficient, placing one foot on the back of the victim, then grabbing their hair and pulling upward with one hand and quickly cutting around the scalp with the other until the hair and scalp was torn clean from the victim's head.

SHOCKING FACT

Scalping

Scalping is the act of removing another's scalp (i.e., skin and hair). It was normally done as a trophy to provide proof of a warrior's prowess in battle. It was also a trophy that could be sold for a bounty as both the English and French paid for prisoners and scalps. Scalping was practiced prior to the arrival of Europeans. Archaeological evidence in North America indicates that scalping was practiced as early as the 14th century. Explorers such as Jacques Cartier in 1535, Hernando de Soto in 1540, and Tristan de Luna in 1559 reported incidents of scalping.

The early writings of the Jesuits portray the shock and horror they felt when they witnessed the display of scalps, the torture of victims, and the practice of cannibalism. Samuel Champlain's observation of his Native allies torturing and subsequently drinking the blood and eating the hearts of their victims, in 1609, caused him a similar revulsion and horror. Not surprisingly, scalping was commonly practiced by combatants during the French and Indian War.

The normal technique for scalping was to place the body on the ground, put a knee between the shoulder blades, and then cut a long arc in the front of the scalp, while maintaining tension by pulling back on the hair. A person could be scalped while dead or alive. Scalping by itself was not a mortal injury.

Courtesy Fort William Henry Corporation.

Provincial Militia.

DID YOU KNOW?

The Good Partisan

In 1759, military theorist Lewis De Jeney explained that a good partisan should possess:

An imagination fertile in schemes, ruses and resource;

A shrewd intelligence, to orchestrate every incident in an action;

A fearless heart in the face of all apparent danger;

A steady countenance, always confident and unmoved by any token of anxiety;

An apt memory; to speak to all by name;

An alert, sturdy, and tireless constitution, to endure all and inspire all;

A rapid and accurate glance, to grasp immediately the defects and advantages, obstacles, and risks presented by a terrain, or by anything it scans; and

Sentiment that will engage the respect, confidence, and affection of everyone.

Other members of the attacking war party struck down or captured individual soldiers who were attempting to escape or run for their muskets. Nate became fixated on one particular unfolding drama. A young soldier stood frozen in fear, still clutching his axe. Overcome by utter terror, the doomed soldier watched as a Native approached and struck him on the head with a tomahawk, splitting his skull wide open. Nate watched as two white men, dressed similar to the others in the war party, entered the centre of the massacre. They quickly shouted out some directions in a language Nate did not understand but assumed was a Native dialect. The surviving British soldiers were rounded up and the dead and wounded were quickly stripped of weapons and clothing. The Natives promptly loaded what they could into the rucksacks that had belonged to the wood-cutting party and forced their prisoners to carry their plunder.

It was obvious the two white men, who Nate reasoned were French-Canadian partisans, were urging their Native allies to hurry, wanting to escape before British soldiers from the fort could rally and come to the rescue of the wood-cutting party. Nate tried to control his breathing; he feared the enemy would hear him. He froze when he realized that two Natives had spotted his axe leaning up against the nearby tree. Nate tried not to panic as they walked toward his hiding place. Another group had already begun to leave the killing ground with their prisoners, leading their human war trophies on a rawhide leash. They quickly disappeared, moving at a running pace.

For a second Nate forgot his own perilous position as he watched his comrades led away to an uncertain fate. Almost too late he realized the two enemy warriors were nearly upon him. He tried to shrink into the ground, willing himself to become small and invisible. The two Natives looked at the axe and then turned to leave. From Nate's position he couldn't see where they went but he was relieved they didn't search the bush around the axe. Just as he began to relax a blood-curdling yell erupted directly behind him — Nate almost jumped out of his skin. He felt himself being grabbed violently by his shirt and pulled from his hiding spot. He was roughly thrown to the ground. As he tried to scramble to his feet he was brutally kicked in the ribs, which forced the air from his lungs, and he collapsed onto the hard, damp ground.

As Nate looked up he saw one of the white partisans looking down at him. "Sir," pleaded Nate, "I am your prisoner of war. Please protect me."

The French Canadian smiled. "You are their prisoner," he stated with a thick accent, "and I suggest you do as they say." He then uttered some words to the Natives and left.

The two Natives quickly motioned to Nate to strip off his clothes. To underline their urgency they began to pull his clothes off him. They then bundled his clothes and shoes together and forced Nate to carry them. Finally, they tied a rawhide rope around his neck. One took the slack end and began to trot down the trail with Nate in tow.

The pace was brisk and Nate had difficulty keeping up. His bare feet quickly became bloody, swollen clumps of flesh as they were torn up running over the brush, rocks, and twigs. He struggled to maintain his balance as he was pulled along. He held on to his bundled clothes and shoes while desperately attempting to watch his footing to avoid stepping on something painful. He fell once and was beaten for his clumsiness.

The pace seemed relentless. They alternated between a run and a brisk walk to distance themselves as much as possible from any rescue force from Fort William Henry. When they reached an inset cove farther down the shoreline of Lake George they quickly loaded into flimsy birch-bark canoes. At this point, Nate gave up all hope of rescue. He now just wanted to survive.

The Natives, who Nate believed to be Abenakis, were clearly skilled at their trade. The two warriors in his canoe stroked in unison. Deep powerful paddle strokes cut clean into the water, raising only the slightest splash. As they pulled back against the water, Nate could feel the canoe shoot forward under the powerful thrust. They picked up more and more speed. Despite the brisk pace the captors seemed impervious to the physical labour.

KEY FACTS

The Abenaki

The Abenaki are First Nations people, members of the Algonquin tribe, whose land extended across northern New England and southern Quebec, as well as the southern Canadian Maritime region. The Abenaki call themselves

Alnôbak, which means "Real People." Although they were originally rooted in New England, frequent wars caused many Abenakis to move to Quebec. They developed a strong alliance with the French and remained staunch allies to the very end. Due to their loyalty to the French and the terror they wrought on the English frontier settlements, Major Robert Rogers and his Rangers mounted a raid on the Abenaki village of St. Francis in 1759.

Finally, after what seemed like hours, the pace of the canoe began to slow. Nate, who was curled up in the centre of the boat, risked raising his head to sneak a peek of his surroundings. He could see they were approaching the mouth of a river with a wide open clearing on the northern shore. As they neared the bank, the captors in his canoe began to "halloo" loudly, which was quickly met by a thunderous reply of yells, shouts, and shrieks from the multitude of Natives who, seemingly from nowhere, assembled along the shore. Overcome with dread, Nate once again began to feel a gnawing pain of fear in his belly.

The warrior in the bow of the canoe deftly jumped out as it entered the shallow, rocky waters close to the bank. He stopped the canoe before it scraped on the rocky bottom of the river to prevent damage to the boat. The warriors then dragged Nate from the watercraft. The cool water actually felt good on his mangled feet, but his relief was fleeting. As he stumbled to shore the gnawing fear grew into foreboding. The devilish reception party who had swarmed to the bank had formed two lines, each facing inward toward the other. Ominously, they left a narrow path running between the two lines.

Nate had heard the terrifying stories of the hardships and tortures endured by those captured by the Natives, who, along with their French-Canadian allies, had become the absolute terror of the frontier. The mere belief that a raiding or ambush party was nearby or especially the sound of the shrill, penetrating war cry would throw even seasoned regular troops into a panic.

As he walked up onto dry land, Nate stopped, hoping somehow to avoid the throng that was yelling and gesturing towards him. His two captors roughly shoved him forward towards the mouth of the sinister gauntlet. From the flank, in broken English, he heard someone yell out, "Anglais, run fast. Run hard if you wish to live." Nate slowly lumbered to face his fate. He hung his head low and walked slowly toward the jeering crowd. However, as he neared the mouth of the opening he suddenly exploded with all his might and speed through the human tunnel. He bent low and protected his head with his arms.

The sudden change in speed surprised his captors and he was able to pass the first dozen warriors with only glancing blows. Their wails of rage were lost on Nate as he concentrated on maintaining speed and balance. But his captors were not to be cheated. Very quickly they recovered and began raining blows on his body with fists and clubs. The lines also closed in so he no longer had clear running space but had to force himself through their powerful muscular bodies. On the verge of unconsciousness he sensed he could see the end of the tunnel, but then he was tripped and fell to the ground. He tried to get up but was repeatedly showered

Library and Archives Canada (LAC), C-69731.

A French-Canadian coureur de bois, seasoned in travelling and fighting in the North American wilderness.

with blows to the point where he stopped trying to get up and just clawed his way forward until he emerged from the other end. He barely felt two of his captors lifting him up off the ground and dragging him to a spot in the middle of the camp where the remainder of the English captives sat tied together in a tight circle facing outward. Nate was unceremoniously dumped in their midst. He promptly fell into unconsciousness.

When Nate awoke he had no idea how long he had been passed out. He could tell that it was late in the day because the sun was in the west and had begun its daily ritual of slipping behind the horizon. Nate groggily sat up and realized he was tethered to the other prisoners. All were naked and covered in bruises and open wounds. Clearly they too had suffered at the hands of the welcoming committee. Two of the prisoners, British regulars who Nate did not personally know, were covered in black soot. The Natives had taken charred wood from their cooking fires and smeared it over the entire bodies of the two soldiers. The ominous feeling of foreboding returned to him, coursing through his body as he realized the fate of the two unfortunate souls. Stories he had heard from those who had escaped their Native captors ran through his head. Nothing seemed crueller than being burnt alive, and if the stories were true, that is exactly what was intended for the two British soldiers.

As darkness enveloped the riverbank, Nate could see a large fire off to his side. Their captors danced around the flames, shouting, yelling, and whooping. Then the inevitable happened: a group of Natives came to fetch the blackened soldiers. They dragged the poor souls off, kicking and screaming the whole way. The soldiers were tied to two posts close to the large fire. The captors took turns taking flaming sticks and burning coals from the fire, which they held to the head, face, hands, and feet of the soldiers.

The soldiers screamed in pain. As the torture continued, hot brands were used to burn more and more of their bodies. When it seemed they could take no more, they threw water on their wounds, which provided only the tiniest bit of relief. Many of the prisoners, who were horrified by the spectacle, whimpered softly. Despite their exhaustion, none could fall into a restful sleep. The cold night air, as well as the horrors they witnessed and fear of what lay ahead kept them awake. The following morning they were claimed by their respective captors and began the long trek to the North, to Canada.

The experience of this small group of prisoners was representative of that of thousands of others who lived along the frontier between New France and the British colonies to the south. Death or captivity were a constant peril. Mercy in the bitter, cruel and savage struggle for the North American wilderness was fleeting. But the stakes could not have been higher. After all, the battle cries in the wilderness would eventually determine the fate of an entire continent.

LAC, C-46282.

Natives torturing a prisoner by fire.

SHOCKING FACT

Torture

The word *torture* is derived from the Latin *tortura*. It is defined as any act that intentionally inflicts pain or suffering, whether physical or mental, on another person.

There were major similarities in the methods of torture used by most Native tribes of the period. These included running the gauntlet, slow burning, application of a necklace of hot tomahawks, piercing of flesh, slicing pieces of flesh for consumption/cannibalism, feeding a captive his own fingers and ears, mutilation, sticking burning torches into flesh, scalping prisoners before death, pouring live coals and hot sand onto scalped head, dissection of body after death, fastening to a stake, and torture of both sexes and all ages. Although there was an element of entertainment involved with torture it also fulfilled a spiritual and emotional need. Torture was often seen as a consolation for the death of a relative or a means of quieting the soul of a deceased. It also provided the means of allowing an enemy to demonstrate his courage. When an opponent was brave, his heart was often eaten because of a belief that it would render those consuming it more courageous.

CHAPTER 1

ADAPT OR DIE

The French Canadians and their allied Natives hadn't always controlled the wilderness of North America. The French Canadians' skill at scouting, raiding, and ambushing — in other words, guerrilla warfare — was learned by necessity. Starting in the early 1600s, and for almost 100 years, they were the targets of Native, mostly Iroquois, raids. For a century the French Canadians suffered war. Eventually, they learned to make war. They came to understand that aggressive offensive action was the best defence for the growing French colony.

From the beginning, the survival of the colonists of New France depended on ingenuity and adaptability. The harsh reality and circumstances of the New World dictated a realistic approach to life in the new French colony. First, New France was a distant wilderness colony in an overtly hostile land. This severely limited its population base, since the constant threat from the Iroquois, and later the English, made it difficult to recruit colonists. For those adventurous enough to venture to the New World, their journey was often marred by hardship and death. Making the situation worse was the fact that New France was not a priority for the French motherland. France was willing to spend only so much to ensure the colony's development and security. France wanted to extract wealth from the New World, not spend money on it. This meant that New France would live or die by its ability to protect itself.

An Iroquois warrior, the scourge of New France.

KEY FACTS

Iroquois

The Iroquois, an indigenous people of North America, are commonly known as the "people of the longhouse." During the 1500s a number of Iroquois tribes came together to form a confederacy (the Five Nations), which consisted of the Cayuga, Oneida, Onondaga, Mohawk, and Seneca tribes. The Tuscarora joined the confederacy (making it the Six Nations) in approximately 1715. The Iroquois were a warlike people whose agricultural base (they grew mostly corn, beans, and squash) allowed them to support a large population as well as expeditionary raids. The Huron viewed the Iroquois as "devil men, who needed nothing, and were hard to kill."

During the French and Indian War, the Iroquois allied themselves with the British against their traditional enemies, the French and their Algonquian allies, although few warriors actually participated with the British on campaigns. During the American Revolution the Iroquois once again sided with the British. After a successful campaign against frontier settlements in 1779, General George Washington ordered a massive offensive against the Iroquois nations to destroy them. When the war ended, a group of Mohawks left New York to settle in Canada. For their service to the Crown they were given a large land grant on the Grand River near present-day Brantford, Ontario. The Iroquois fought once again with the British during the War of 1812.

As a result, the inhabitants and leaders of New France developed a way of war that reflected their environment, their capability, and their temperament. They could not afford to fight for extended periods of time or suffer many casualties, since their population was so small. They had to learn how to fight and survive in the wilderness of North America.

SHOCKING REALITY

A Shortage of Colonists

Initially, very few settlers ventured to the New World. By the middle of the 17th century there were only approximately 2,500 people in New France. Many of them were explorers, fur traders, and missionaries. But the lure of freedom, opportunity, and especially wealth was enough of a draw to generate growth and the French established settlements and a series of forts, mostly for fur trading.

LAC, C- 6643.

Samuel de Champlain, the governor of New France, and his Native allies defeated an Iroquois war party near the present town of Ticonderoga, New York, on July 30, 1609.

Simply put, it was a matter of adapt or die. Compared to Europe, the Canadian climate was harsh. The thick, deep forests seemed impossible to penetrate and the Natives, especially the Iroquois, were hostile. The French colonists had to make alliances. For this reason, Samuel de Champlain, the first governor of New France, quickly entered into treaties of friendship and trading partnerships with a number of northern tribes such as the Abenaki, Algonquin, Huron, Montagnais, and Outaouais. Champlain did this even though he knew that many of these tribes were locked in conflict with the far more aggressive Iroquois confederacy. His decision had serious consequences and eventually made war inescapable.

KEY FACTS

Samuel de Champlain

Samuel de Champlain was a French navigator, cartographer, draughtsman, soldier, explorer, geographer, diplomat, and writer. He is known as the "Father of New France."

Champlain was born into a family of master mariners and began exploring North America in 1603 under the tutelage of François Gravé Du Pont, a navigator and merchant. Champlain was part of the expedition that explored and settled Acadia from 1604–07. The following year, in July 1608, he founded Quebec City. In his determination to protect French settlements in New France, he entered into a series of alliances with local tribes that brought France into conflict with the Iroquois, which led to almost a century of fighting.

He was captured by the English in 1629, after a siege of Quebec City, but returned to New France in 1633 as the governor. His great success in establishing a fur trading organization that was economically viable laid the foundations of New France's development. Champlain suffered a severe stroke in October 1635, and passed two months later. He was buried in Quebec City, although the exact site is not known.

However, the attack was a great success. On July 30, 1609, Champlain led a combined French, Algonquin, and Huron force, the first of its kind, against the Iroquois at a site near present-day Ticonderoga, New York. Armed with an arquebus (an early type of musket), with his first shot Champlain killed two Iroquois chiefs and injured a third warrior. His two French companions, also equipped with firearms, opened fire from the flank. This caused the Iroquois to panic, particularly because of the weapons they'd not yet encountered, and they fled. The following year, Champlain and his allies also drove an Iroquois war party out of the Richelieu Valley.

Although these early victories impressed the Natives allied to the French, they would prove to be costly. The defeats were humiliating to the proud Iroquois confederacy, who then became unforgiving enemies of the French. This led to almost a century of conflict. By 1627, the Iroquois had become a constant terror to the colonists, threatening the very survival of New France.

The threat to the colony was not surprising. The Iroquois were very effective warriors and had a lot of practise fighting in the forests of North America. They forced the colonists to barricade themselves in cramped stockades, only venturing out to tend their fields in large armed groups. Even then, there was no guarantee of safety. "The Iroquois used to keep us closely confined," wrote one Jesuit missionary, "that we did not even dare till the lands that were under the cannon of the forts." One early Canadian historian recorded that "no white man could venture beyond the settlement without incurring great danger … Buildings languished, and much of the cleared land remained uncultivated." A French governor described,

> They are everywhere. They will stay hidden behind a stump for ten days, existing on nothing but a handful of corn, waiting to kill a man, or a woman … the Iroquois are not content to burn the houses, they also burn the prisoners they take, and

give them death only after torturing them continually in the most cruel manner they can devise … it was the cruellest war in the world.

Even the arrival of French soldiers did not improve the situation. Although they established garrisons in some locations, there were not enough troops to cover the entire colony. More importantly, the French soldiers could not match the skill of the Iroquois in the North American wilderness. In fact, the Iroquois control over the French was so one-sided that an Iroquois chief boasted, "We plied the French homes in the war with them that they were not able to go out a door to piss." In the end, the situation did not improve. "The Iroquois," declared King Louis the XIV of France, "through massacres and inhumanities, have prevented the country's population from growing."

It is not surprising that the constant hardship and terror inflicted on the growing French-Canadian population shaped their collective experience and outlook. It made them more stoic and courageous, and gave them a ruggedness and strength that allowed them to stand up to the hardships of the North American wilderness. It also ingrained in them a level of ferocity and savageness that made others fear them. In the end, the French Canadians adopted a Native way of making war, based on a tactical outlook dependent on the clever use of ground and cover, the element of surprise, sudden ambush, and swift raids. It also led them to only engage in combat if there was a good chance of winning without a lot of casualties.

This mentality evolved slowly — at first, few settlers ventured to the New World. The French-Canadian colonists and coureurs de bois studied under their Native allies and learned the ways of the land. They lived with the Natives and learned their culture and language. They forged tight bonds that would develop trade, social, and military relationships. They learned how to dress, travel, and navigate over the large expanses of wilderness in all seasons. They also learned

LAC, C-19,253.

The French used forts and outposts to lock their hold on the allegiance of their Native allies since the forts fulfilled two functions: one, they demonstrated military strength and two, they served as trading posts.

how to survive in the vast, harsh wilderness of North America, which was the most important skill.

With time, the French Canadians developed a confidence and mastery over their environment. They also studied their enemy, the Iroquois. Then, in 1665, with the arrival of a large reinforcement of 1,400 French regular soldiers, mainly from the Carignan-Salières Regiment, the opportunity finally came to strike back. The leaders in New France developed a strategy to protect the colony and defeat their mortal enemy.

Lieutenant-General Alexandre de Prouville de Tracy, the senior French military commander assigned the task of defeating the Iroquois menace, quickly developed a plan of action. First, he decided to deny the Iroquois access to the vital waterways that led into New France. He built forts at strategic locations to close off the Richelieu Valley from Lake Champlain to the St. Lawrence River. These forts filled an important economic and political purpose by controlling access to major waterways and acting as trade outlets. This reinforced French territorial claims and power in the New World. They also provided a presence within the wilderness that was recognized and accessed by the various Native nations. They became a key component of the French hold on their Native allies.

KEY FACTS

Coureurs de bois

The government of New France attempted to regulate the trade with the Indians. They prohibited traders from going into "Indian Country" without a licence. However, licences were only granted to a few traders, in an attempt to maximize profits for those in positions of power. The coureurs de bois were the unlicenced fur traders who escaped into the wilderness of North America and lived with the Indians. Many young men in the colony were lured by the promise of adventure and fortune in the wilds, as well as the ease and freedom of life in the Indian villages. Toward the end of the 1600s, historians estimate that as many as one-third of the able-bodied men of New France were coureurs de bois. These "runners of the woods" contributed significantly to the development of the fur trade and exploration of Canada. They also cemented Indian alliances to the French and provided expertise in wilderness travel and fighting.

The forts denied the Iroquois easy access into New France, particularly through the use of the Richelieu Valley waterway, allowing the French to intercept Iroquois war parties. At a minimum, the forts forced the enemy to seek alternate routes by either land and/or water, extending the distances that an enemy would have to travel and, subsequently, the time needed to execute attacks on the settlements.

DID YOU KNOW?

The Carignan-Salières Regiment

The Carignan-Salières Regiment was formed in 1659. In 1664, King Louis XIV decided to put an end to the Iroquois attacks on New France. The following spring, he sent the regiment to New France. Approximately 1,200 soldiers and 80 officers, under the command of General Alexandre de Prouville, Sieur de Tracy, left La Rochelle, France, on seven ships in May 1665. They arrived in Quebec four months later.

The Regiment was divided into 24 companies. They built and manned a series of forts along the important interior waterways and mounted two operations against the Iroquois that resulted in a tentative peace between the two sides. As a result of the peace the Regiment was recalled to France in 1668. Of the approximate 1,280 members that landed in 1665, 446 settled in Canada and 200 returned to France.

Finally, the forts also provided the French forces with a secure forward-operating position. The French forces and their Canadian militia and Native allies could now function more easily at a distance from the settled areas. In essence, the forts represented the first line of defence for New France — a defence that was based on fighting on the outer frontier of the colony or beyond it. They could now attempt to contain the violence and destruction to the frontier regions. More importantly, the forts acted as launching pads to conduct offensive operations. They provided assembly points and supply

LAC, C-10368.

In 1665, the King of France deployed 1,400 regular soldiers from the Carignan-Salières Regiment to battle the Iroquois threat to the colony.

depots prior to setting off into enemy territory. At long last, the French and Canadians could conduct war elsewhere — they could fight away to protect their home. The offence could now be practised as the most effective form of defence. The inhabitants of New France could now strike at the Iroquois on their own terms, in their own territory.

The first opportunity to try out this new strategy occurred in January 1666, during the height of the vicious North American winter. Daniel de Rémy de Courcelle, the governor of New France, personally led 300 regular troops from the Carignan-Salières Regiment. The deep snow and freezing temperatures took a severe toll. Freezing rain, inadequate winter clothing, and a lack of snowshoes just added to the misery. The European troops suffered terribly due to the harsh conditions. However, the approximately 200 Canadians and the handful of friendly Natives who accompanied them did not. The ability and strength of the French Canadians and their Native allies made a huge impression on the expedition leader. He quickly realized that they were at home in the woods and were capable warriors in wilderness fighting. He made great use of them. They acted as scouts and the forward combat element during the approach march. During the withdrawal and return to New France they were used as the rear-guard to protect the regular forces from any Iroquois pursuit. In all subsequent expeditions, as a point of principle, large contingents of Canadians were always included as a key component of the fighting force.

In the end, the expedition actually failed. It did not meet its objective of destroying or humbling the Iroquois — specifically the Mohawks, who were one of the tribes in the Iroquois confederacy. The French expedition did not locate any Mohawk villages and they only destroyed a few outlying cabins. Furthermore, only four Iroquois warriors were killed and six others wounded, compared to seven French troops killed and four wounded in the skirmish with the Mohawks. There were, nonetheless, approximately 400 French casualties in all; most of these were attributed to hypothermia and starvation.

KEY FACTS

Canadian Militia

With a population of only 60,000, New France faced the danger of being engulfed by its larger neighbour to the south, the English colonies, where approximately 1,500,000 people lived. The threat was enormous. During the French and Indian War, the English colonies outnumbered New France in manpower by nearly 25 to one.

Luckily for the French, they had created a militia decades earlier. All Canadian men between the ages of 16 and 60, who were fit to bear arms, had to join the militia. Companies were based on the same framework as a regular French company. Each militia company was commanded by a captain and assisted by a lieutenant and an ensign, as well as a number of non-commissioned officers (corporals and sergeants). The companies were approximately 50-men strong. Each parish provided a company, or more, depending on its size. Their fieldcraft skills made them irreplaceable. One British commander noted that the Canadians travelled without baggage and that they supported and maintained themselves in the woods. He concluded that they "do more execution than four or five time their number of our men."

Despite the less-than-hoped-for results, the first expedition against the Iroquois represented a significant turning point. It demonstrated that expeditions, even at the worst time of the year, when operations were normally never conducted by either side, were possible. Moreover, the French Canadians proved themselves to be masters at travelling, surviving, and fighting in the trackless forests.

A second French foray took place that autumn. This time, the force was substantially larger. It was made up of approximately 600 regular soldiers and an equal number of Canadian volunteers, as well as about 100 Natives. The second expedition was marginally more successful than the first. The operation lasted two months and failed to bring the Mohawks to decisive battle. However, it did succeed in deploying a large French force into the heart of Mohawk territory, where they destroyed four Mohawk villages and their crops and stored foodstuffs, which the expedition leaders estimated could "nourish all Canada for two entire years." As a result, the Iroquois were forced to endure a slow death by starvation and exposure over the winter, or the humiliating prospect of begging for food from other tribes or their English allies.

Not surprisingly, the French achieved their aim. The bold strikes brought their enemies to the peace table. The Iroquois, now faced with an enemy that was capable of launching attacks into their territory and wreaking terror and destruction on their homes, quickly decided to sue for peace.

DID YOU KNOW?

Pyrrhic Victory

A pyrrhic victory is a success on the battlefield that is offset by staggering losses. The term was derived from the experience of King Pyrrhus of Epirus, whose army defeated the Romans at Heraclea in 280 BC, and at Asculum in 279 BC, during the Pyrrhic War.

However, his armies suffered irreplaceable casualties as a result of the victories, including his best officers. King Pyrrhus was quoted as saying something like, "If we are victorious in one more battle with the Romans, we shall be utterly ruined." The point was, although the Romans lost the battles and suffered greater casualties, they had a larger pool of soldiers to draw from so the defeats had little impact on their war effort.

King Pyrrhus' losses were crippling, despite the fact that he was victorious.

In sum, the expeditions had an important psychological effect on the Iroquois and the French. Their larger resources, string of fortifications, discipline, firepower, and willingness and ability to fight in the wilderness made them more imposing foes. For the Canadians, the expeditions also underlined the importance and effectiveness of offensive action. Furthermore, they gave the volunteers military experience and the regulars wilderness training. But most importantly, the expeditions highlighted the inherent strength of utilizing the Canadians, who were adept at living, travelling, and fighting in the Native fashion in North America. In short, it was the practical and functional aspect that gave the Canadians a martial value, as well as their acquired field skills.

KEY FACTS

Compagnies Franches de la Marine

Compagnies Franches de la Marine were created by King Louis XIV in December 1690, as independent companies of the navy. In essence, they were French colonial regular infantry soldiers raised in company strength to guard naval ports in France and to serve overseas in the French colonies. They were under the control of the Ministry of Marine (Navy), rather than the Ministry of War, to avoid the problems in the regimental system of the army at that time. For this reason they were independent companies and not part of existing regiments.

Commissions in the Compagnies Franches de la Marine were not purchased, which was common at the time, they were earned by merit (although they were also affected by influence of important people). Each company was commanded by a captain, and consisted of a lieutenant, a brevet ensign, a second ensign, two cadets, two sergeants, three corporals, two drummers, and 41 soldiers. In 1756, the strength of the non-commissioned ranks per company was increased to 65.

Increasingly, Canadians began to serve as officers in the *Compagnies Franches de la Marine*. The colonial troops did not offer much in the way of advancement for regular French officers (since each company was commanded by only a captain), so positions were often difficult to fill. Vacancies were given to individuals from the Canadian gentry or to the families of French officers who remained in Canada. This became common practice.

The result of those expeditions was a long period of peace. The leaders of New France quickly seized on the success of their new strategy and made it the pattern for future operations. But the French Canadians and their Native allies were the ones who became responsible for this new aggressive, offensive strategy. After all, they were the ones who proved themselves so capable in the wilderness. The two early expeditions against the Iroquois had an important psychological effect on the French Canadians. First, the raids demonstrated the importance and effectiveness of offensive action. The raids showed the success of striking the enemy where they lived. The expeditions also gave the volunteers military experience and the regulars troops wilderness indoctrination. Of greatest consequence, the expeditions provided the French Canadians with self-confidence in military operations. Their ability became so well-respected that in April 1669, King Louis XIV ordered Governor Courcelle to organize a Canadian militia.

The King of France directed that men in the colony "always be well armed and always have the powder, lead, and fuses necessary to use their arms when needed." As a result, all men between the ages of 16 and 60 who were fit to bear arms were compelled to join the militia. Militia companies were based on the same framework as a regular company in the French military. Each company was commanded by a captain, who was assisted by a lieutenant and an ensign, as well as a number of non-commissioned officers (corporals and sergeants).

The companies were approximately 50-men strong. Within New France, each church parish provided a company or more, depending on its size.

The importance of the militia became increasingly significant. By 1668 the Carignan-Salières Regiment was sent home to France. The defence of New France was once again largely left in the hands of a few scattered regular and colonial troops and the French-Canadian settlers.

CHAPTER 2

THE CANADIAN
WAY OF WAR

The return of the Carignan-Salières Regiment to France did not overly concern the French Canadians. By the end of 17th century they had become confident in their abilities. "Our youth is hardened and quite used to the woods," boasted one official in New France. "We make war better than the Iroquois and English."

The French official was right. The French Canadians had become very capable fighters, much to the dismay of the English and their Iroquois allies to the south. From 1688 to 1748, raids by combined war parties of French colonial troops, French Canadians, and their allied Natives terrorized the frontier. The French raiding parties attacked targets such as the English in Hudson Bay, the Iroquois in New York State, and a large number of English settlements along the frontier, such as Casco, Deersfield, Haverhill, Salmon Falls, and Schenectady.

The leadership of New France had learned the hard lesson rooted in generations of struggle: an opponent who is focused on defending his home is less likely, and less able, to attack you. They also realized that they could mobilize a series of devastating raids faster than the English could organize an invasion of New France. And the raids were devastating. Their savageness and ferocity struck utter terror in the hearts and minds of the English living on the frontier. "Nothing," stated the Canadian-born governor of New France, Pierre de Rigaud de Vaudreuil, "is more calculated to discourage the people of these English colonies and make them wish for the return to peace [than our raids]."

SHOCKING REALITY

The Natives as Allies

Although Native allies provided many advantages, they came at a price. European commanders characterized the Natives as an unwanted burden, if not a nuisance. "They drive us crazy from morning to night," exclaimed one senior French officer. "There is no end to their demands ... in short one needs the patience of an angel with these devils, and yet one must always force himself to seem pleased with them," he concluded.

Colonel Bougainville complained, "One must be the slave to these savages, listen to them day and night, in council and in private, whenever the fancy takes them, or whenever a dream or a fit of vapours, or their perpetual craving for brandy, gets possession of them; besides which they are always wanting something for their equipment, arms, or toilet." In an attempt not to upset the Natives the most outrageous offences were accepted. One French officer decried the tolerance shown to their Native allies. "You could see them running throughout Montreal," he wrote, "knife in hand, threatening and insulting everyone." Governors of New France, particularly Vaudreuil, were constantly criticized for their leniency towards the Natives. Out of 76 Natives accused of disorderly conduct, assault, or murder in the Montreal district alone, between 1669 and 1760, only one man was actually prosecuted. The rest were released without charge. The rationale was simple, though unpleasant for the French and Canadians — the authorities feared that the harsh justice demanded by the French criminal code would alienate the Natives and cause them to defect to the British.

Their behaviour on campaigns was little better. Montcalm confided to his journal that "[the Natives] feeling the need we have of them, are extremely insolent; they wish our fowls this evening. They took with force some barrels of wine, killed some cattle, and it is necessary to endure all." French officers claimed that it was very expensive to maintain their Native allies because they "exhausted so much provisions" and "could not be stinted to allowance taking everything at pleasure and destroying three times the Quantity of Provisions they could eat." The Natives had no sense of rationing and would consume a week's worth of provisions in three days then demand more. Consistently, the Europeans denounced the Natives as disruptive to their campaigns and a drain on valuable resources. "One is a slave to Natives in this country," lamented Bougainville, but he also added that "they are a necessary evil." In the end, both French and English regular officers preferred a disciplined force of Europeans capable of ranging duties instead of Natives, Canadians, or American Rangers.

DID YOU KNOW?

Pierre de Rigaud de Vaudreuil

Pierre de Rigaud de Vaudreuil was born in Quebec on November 22, 1698. He was the son of Philippe de Rigaud Marquis de Vaudreuil, the governor of New France. At the age of six he was commissioned as an ensign in *Les Compagnies Franche de la Marine*. He attained the rank of lieutenant at 13 and captain at 15. He served on an expedition to fight the Fox tribe in 1728 and five years later was appointed governor of Trois-Rivières. In 1742, he became the governor of Louisiana.

Vaudreuil proved to be a very capable military officer and administrator. In 1753 he was appointed governor of New France. Canadian-born and raised, he fully understood the Canadian way of war and used his irregular forces to raid and harass the frontier settlements to continually preempt, disrupt, and keep the British on the defensive. As long as he outranked his military commander-in-chief, Major-General Montcalm, he was able to execute his strategy. However, after the victory at Fort Ticonderoga and the promotion of Montcalm to lieutenant-general, Montcalm became the senior-ranking officer and changed strategies, deciding to gamble the fate of New France on a concentrated defence at the gates of Quebec City. The French forces were defeated on the Plains of Abraham in September 1759, and the French surrendered New France on September 8, 1760. On return to France, Vaudreuil retired to his estates in France, where he resided until his death in 1778.

New France had developed a definite strategy, a clearly Canadian way of war, to fight for control of the North American wilderness. Many of the French and Canadian leaders, particularly those born and raised in Canada who had an extended exposure to the North American manner of war, developed what they believed to be the optimum war-fighting organization. It consisted of a mixed force that included regular French troops, French-Canadian militia, and Natives. The regulars provided traditional military strengths such as courage, discipline, and tactical know-how. The French-Canadian volunteers and Native allies brought with them endurance, familiarity with wilderness navigation, travel, and survival, as well as marksmanship. The French Canadians relied more on their own initiative and independent action rather than on rigid military practise and drill. This made them more dangerous because they were unpredictable and creative in their approach to war. In short, they practiced *la petite guerre*.

LAC, C-3708.

Pierre de Rigaud, Marquis de Vaudreuil, governor of New France. Vaudreuil relied heavily on the Canadian way of war to maintain the security of New France.

The ability to endure the harsh climate, navigate the vast hinterland, and fight in the Native way made Canadians a dreaded foe.

"Soldier Dressed for Winter Campaign," by Francis Back © Parks Canada.

La petite guerre, which means "small war," was small-scale irregular warfare. The key to its success was selecting only a few targets that could be easily beaten. Stealth and surprise were the most important thing — ambushes and raids were the preferred method of attack. Lightning strikes were always followed by immediate withdrawals. Unfortunately, these operations did not achieve much. They only disrupted or delayed the enemy's attacks. The basic idea was to hit the enemy when and where they least expected it, before they could strike at you. By doing that, the enemy would be constantly thrown off balance and kept in a weakened condition. This would prevent them from being able to attack New France.

This followed the Native way of war. Tecaughretanego, a famous Kahnawake chief, explained, "The art of war consists in ambushing and surprising our enemies, and in preventing them from ambushing and surprising us." A Jesuit missionary, Father Nau, observed that the Native "mode of warfare is but stratagem and surprise."

DID YOU KNOW?

Jesuits

Jesuits is the name given to members of the Society of Jesus, a religious order of the Roman Catholic Church. It was founded by Ignatius of Loyola, who, with six others, took vows of poverty and chastity while students in Paris. He named his group Companã de Jess, which in Spanish means Company of Jesus. Pope Paul III approved the order in 1540 and it began to expand.

Jesuits believe that saving souls is their main purpose in life. Therefore, they took on the challenge of converting newly discovered populations in the New World. Jesuit missionaries travelled to New France to convert the Natives to Christianity. Their efforts often put them in direct opposition to the government and other Roman Catholic clergy. The "Black-Robes," as they were called by the Natives, made great inroads with the Hurons and had some success with the Iroquois. Nonetheless, a number of Jesuits were martyred as they attempted to convert the North American Natives.

Today the society has approximately 24,000 members.

The way the Natives fought took full advantage of their knowledge of the terrain and forests. Jesuit missionary Pierre Roubaud wrote, "The woods are the element of the Savages; they run through them with the swiftness of a deer." They used the cover of tree and bushes to its fullest benefit, deliberately choosing not to make themselves an obvious target. According to the Natives themselves, they gained the upper hand by travelling alone, instead of in groups, making themselves less obvious targets. "The English always kept in a heap together [so] that it was as easy to hit them, as to hit a house." In fact, the Natives felt that the way the white men fought was ineffective because the soldiers formed in close ranks, presenting such a large target that they were almost impossible to miss. Meanwhile, the Natives remained thinly scattered, concealing themselves behind bushes or trees so that they were hard to see and shoot at.

Colonel Henry Bouquet, at the time a recognized expert on Native fighting, concluded that Native warriors were "physically active, fierce in manner, skilful in the use of weapons, and capable of great guile and stealth in combat." He considered them formidable opponents. "So stealthy in their approach, so swift in their execution, and so expeditious in their retreat," wrote a Jesuit missionary, "that one commonly learns of their [Natives] departure before being aware of their arrival."

Colonel Isaac Barré, another officer who served in colonial North America, felt that as enemies the Natives were "the most subtile [*sic*] and the most formidable of any people upon the face of God's earth." Bouquet concluded,

"Native tactics in battle could be reduced to three principles: surround the enemy, fight in scattered formation, and always give ground when attacked."

SHOCKING REALITY

War — The Ultimate Hunt?

The Natives way of fighting was similar to their hunting methods. The skills needed for a successful hunt (stealth, surprise, marksmanship) are also good for combat in the forests of North America. To ensure game was killed required exceptional fieldcraft skills; the more clever and stealthy the hunter, the greater his chances of success. Clearly, all these skills were transferable to war-making.

Firearms just made things more efficient and deadly. The Natives often carved grooves into the stock of their weapons so that they could take better aim by aligning their eyes along the barrel of their musket in line with their target. This was because neither the French Charleville .69 calibre musket, nor the British .75 calibre "Brown Bess" musket had rear sights, as the Europeans felt they were unnecessary because of the perceived inaccuracy of the smoothbore musket and the reliance on volley fire.

The success of the Natives also depended on the element of surprise, their ease in moving through the forest, and their excellent marksmanship. In fact, many French and English commanders felt that it was the Natives' excellent aim that made them such a threat. They always aimed at single targets, specifically at officers who were easy to identify by their clothing and position on the battlefield. Captain Pierre Pouchot, a member of the French Béarn Regiment that fought with distinction in North America, wrote in his memoirs that the Natives were excellent marksmen who "very rarely fail to shoot their man down."

From L'Abbé Casgrain, *Les Français au Canada*. (Quebec: Maison Alfred Mame et Fils, undated.)

A French-Canadian partisan and his Native allies.

But it was not just their fieldcraft or marksmanship that set the Natives apart from the Europeans. There was a cultural and philosophical component that was not always understood. For Native warriors, "taking up the hatchet" — simply put, going to war — was a personal decision. War was important to warriors because they had to prove their courage and skill in combat to obtain prestige. That is why taking prisoners, scalps, and plunder was so important. It was proof of a warrior's courage and success in battle.

Warriors were free agents who did not have to report to anyone. They saw neither shame nor dishonour in abandoning the field of battle if the odds of easy success were against them. Abbé H.R. Casgrain, a prominent French-Canadian historian in the 1800s, explained, "For them [Natives], withdrawal was not a flight, nor a disgrace, it was a means of falling back to occupy a better position."

If a warrior left because they got tired of the campaign, or just didn't agree with what the other warriors were doing, the other warriors usually did not get upset with them. Warriors were not interested in a fair fight — only in winning with a minimum of casualties. For that reason, ambush, raids, and terror were their preferred way of fighting a war.

This form of warfare was perfect for the Canadians. After all, necessity had forced them to learn the Native way of fighting, and they had gotten good at it. The Canadians and their Native allies quickly earned a reputation for barbarity and savageness. The English blamed Governor Vaudreuil, who they saw as the architect of the terror being inflicted on the frontier settlements. But Vaudreuil was not about to give up such an effective strategy. The deep strikes into English territory during the French and Indian War, which was the North American component of the Seven Years' War, consistently disrupted British campaign plans and kept the English on the defensive from the summer of 1755 until 1758. It ravaged frontier settlements, economies, and public morale.

KEY FACTS

The European Way of War
The Europeans arrived in North America with preconceived ideas of how war should be fought. European armies consisted mainly of conscripted men and social outcasts, and were mostly led by the country's aristocracy. There was

little keeping these two groups together. While the officer corps may have had a reason to fight for king and country because of their position in the society, their soldiers did not — their allegiance was to themselves. They did not fight for an ideological, political, or philosophical cause. Their primary focus was to make a living. Soldiers were not expected, or trusted, to operate as individuals or small groups because of their commanders' fear that they would desert or create havoc, regardless of whether they were in friendly or enemy territory. Major-General James Wolfe wrote, "I have a very mean opinion of the infantry in general. I know their discipline to be bad, & their valour precarious. They are easily put into disorder & hard to recover out of it; they frequently kill their Officers thro' fear, & murder one another in their confusion." This was one reason why commanders used only large formations in combat to ensure the troops remained in their place of duty and fought. This lack of cohesion within an army, and the absence of a clear purpose that the soldiers could identify with, also made it necessary for army leaders to rely on iron discipline to create a unified, effective fighting force.

The need for harsh discipline also extended to the type of combat that the soldiers conducted. This was also another driving force behind the use of large formations. The weapons of the day were not very effective, particularly the fourteen-pound .75 calibre smoothbore flintlock Long Land Pattern Musket, affectionately called the "Brown Bess." It was usually 46 inches long, not very accurate, and only useful at short range. Although capable of firing up to 300 yards, the Brown Bess was best for ranges less than 100 yards. Reloading lasted about 30 to 40 seconds and the average soldier could reload approximately two times per minute. However, a musket would typically misfire three to four times out of every 25 loadings. Furthermore, after 50 to 100 loadings it would be useless unless the firer carefully cleaned out the vent, swabbed the barrel, and inserted new flints.

During combat, battalions stood elbow to elbow in a solid line, three ranks deep, facing a mirror image of themselves no more than 30 to 80 metres away. On a given command, volleys would be exchanged with devastating effect on the closely packed formations. Soldiers in the ranks rarely took specific aim. The winners were the side that could deliver the most volleys in the shortest possible time and not break and run. At 80 paces there was little time to reload. If a volley did not strike home it could lead to a bayonet charge by the enemy. As a result, repetitive training was required to turn the soldiers into an efficient fighting force. Loading and firing a musket required approximately 12 movements, all of which were coordinated by drum beat or on word of command by an officer. Normally, it took at least 18 months on the drill square to train the raw recruit to manoeuvre and perform effectively on the battlefield. But equally important was severe discipline to ensure that soldiers maintained the advance under murderous fire, or simply remained in position. One great commander stated that a soldier "must be more afraid of his officers than of the dangers to which he is exposed." It was not uncommon for regulations to specifically emphasize that "if a soldier during an action looks about as if to flee, or so much as sets foot outside the line, the non-commissioned officer standing behind him will run him through with his bayonet and kill him on the spot."

Therefore, the European battle model became an elaborate set-piece manoeuvre. Formations of artillery, cavalry, and infantry were carefully deployed and repositioned to gain the maximum amount of advantage over the enemy. Tactics relied almost exclusively on heavy infantry and cavalry. The courage of the soldiers to withstand the murderous volleys of the enemy was maintained by an iron discipline. The ability to pour a withering fire into the opponents ranks was honed by constant drilling and training. The soldier was in many ways seen by his commanders as nothing more than an expendable automaton — but an expensive one to train.

The raids terrorized the frontier and tied down large numbers of Anglo troops, who had to stay close to the settlements to provide security. The plight of the English colonists could not be ignored by their political leaders. The incursions into Virginia alone caused the governor there to raise 10 militia companies, a total of 1,000 men, for internal defence. Similarly, Pennsylvania raised 1,500 provincial troops and built a string of forts from New Jersey to Maryland in an attempt to impede the Canadian raiders. The forts had to be staffed with soldiers and resources that subsequently could not be used to invade New France.

KEY FACTS

The Strategic Importance of Forts

The French reliance on a series of fortifications on the frontiers of the colony to control access to waterways leading into New France was key to their ability to maintain control of New France. These strategically positioned forts were symbols of power, as well as important economic, political, and social centres that cemented Native alliances. But more importantly, they were imposing barriers that provided a buffer between hostile territory and the French settlements. Their strategic locations allowed a relatively small force to delay, or stop altogether, the advances of a much larger and stronger antagonist. These wilderness sentinels also forced would-be invaders to lengthen their lines of communication and supply, exposing them to constant attack by irregulars. The forts were also a key part of Vaudreuil's strategy because they acted as springboards for offensive strikes deep into enemy territory. The forts allowed for forward defence — namely, a fight-away policy. Raiding parties could be sent from the forts to devastate the New England frontier and strike terror in the hearts and minds of their antagonists.

The English militiamen were reluctant to go and fight the French and Canadians when they felt their families were at risk. And the destruction of settlements, farms, and livestock, as well as the murder or capture of settlers, ate away at the economy of the English colonies. Crops could not be sown or harvested; grains could not be stored for the winter, or be used to feed the army on campaign. Both soldier and citizen were deprived of the necessities of life. The impact on the frontier was, quite simply, shattering.

One English colonist complained:

> We are under the utmost fear and consternation … Accounts of the Natives having again began their murders and massacres in the province of Pennsylvania, upon the River Delaware adjoining to this province … These fresh depredations have so terrified us that we dare not go out to our daily labour, for fear of being surprised and murdered by the Natives.

An English officer angrily decried that:

> Nothing is to be seen but desolation and murder, heightened with every barbarous circumstance, and new instances of cruelty … They [the Natives], at the instigation of the French with them, burn up the plantations, the smoke of which darkens the day and hides the mountains from our sight.

Laments like those were widespread.

The accounts were backed up by the French. Claude-Godefroy Coquart, a French priest, wrote his brother, "Our Natives have waged the most cruel war against the English … Georgia, Carolina, Maryland, Pennsylvania, are wholly laid waste … The [English] farmers have been forced to quit their abodes and to retire into the town … They have neither ploughed nor planted."

But this was precisely what Governor Vaudreuil wanted. It was, after all, in keeping with the Canadian way of war in North America. Not only were the raids effective, more importantly, they were relatively cheap. Raiding required limited resources. Small parties of warriors, led by French or Canadian officers and consisting of skilled Natives and militia, could cause as much damage as a far larger group. These raiders could also tie up considerably larger enemy forces by forcing them to protect settlements from enemy attacks. The raids, just as had happened with the French Canadians, forced the English to surrender the initiative and remain on the defensive.

This manner of fighting a war — that is, a defensive war — is simply unacceptable. It makes everyone suffer, especially civilians. After all, it is nearly impossible to protect everyone, everywhere, all the time. "What can one do against invisible enemies who strike and flee with the rapidity of light?" asked French Colonel Louis Antoine Comte de Bougainville. He answered his own question: "It is the destroying angel."

For the French Canadians and their Native allies, the Canadian way of war was ideal. It allowed them to compensate for their small numbers. It also allowed them to choose when and where to strike and ensured they always had enough men at home during the critical fall harvest.

The evidence of the Canadians' effectiveness was in the fear they created in their enemies. Statements by British generals and other accounts agreed that the Canadian raiders were "well known to be the most dangerous enemy of any … reckoned equal, if not superior in that part of the world to veteran troops." The constant Canadian ambushes and raids were a material and economic drain on the British. They were also an overwhelming psychological and moral blow against the Anglo-American colonies. The British forces seemed unable to strike back. They suffered a constant series of defeats and each of their

Painting by Ted Zuber.

intended campaigns was thwarted. Everywhere, the Canadians and Natives would appear, like phantoms. Their hit-and-run attacks left smouldering ruins and bodies of the dead and dying in their wake. The result was an utterly paralyzing effect on the English combatants and colonists alike.

The skill and effectiveness of the Canadians could not be denied. French Colonel Bougainville wrote, "God knows we do not wish to disparage the value of the Canadians … In the woods, behind trees, no troops are comparable to the natives of this country." The official journals kept by the French Army in

Fort St. Frédéric was used as a launching pad for raiding parties that terrorized the English frontier settlements.

North America revealed, "The Canadians … certainly surpass all the troops in the universe, owing to their skill as marksmen."

Even their enemies had to agree. British Major-General James Wolfe felt that "every man in Canada is a soldier." Many English officers echoed the sentiment that the Canadian woodsmen and coureurs de bois were "well known to be the most dangerous enemy of any … reckoned equal, if not superior in that part of the world to veteran troops."

So the French-Canadian and Native allies developed a distinct Canadian way of war, tailored specifically for the struggle for the North American wilderness. The objective was not to capture territory or destroy the enemy's army. Rather, it was to terrorize the enemy population into seeking peace as the only alternative to the terrifying raids. It was also designed to keep the English from trying to invade or strike at New France. The strategy was an inexpensive way to maintain the balance of power in North America and protect the French settlements from the ravages of war. It was a strategy that was born from a relative position of weakness. For decades it had worked efficiently, giving New France a military strength inconsistent with its size or actual economic or political capacity. However, it did not make the English consider peace, as Governor Vaudreuil had hoped it would. Instead, the English decided it was time for them to adapt.

SHOCKING REALITY

Braddock's Defeat

No battle was a better example of the Canadian way of war than the crushing defeat of Major-General Edward Braddock at the Monongahela River on July 9, 1755. Braddock, who was the newly appointed commander-in-chief of British forces in North America, had a force of approximately 1,200 regular and 800 provincial soldiers. He was en route to capture Fort Duquesne, a strategic western outpost held by the French in the Ohio Valley. However, he was intercepted and soundly defeated by a smaller force of 250 French regulars and militia and 600 Natives.

Before he left, Braddock dismissed the threat posed by the Canadians and Natives. He declared that "these savages may, indeed, be a formidable enemy to your raw American militia, but upon the King's regulars ... it is impossible they should make any impression." Braddock believed that British courage, training, and discipline would defeat such a motley group of irregulars. However, as Braddock's force neared the fort, they were ambushed by the French, Canadians, and Natives. Dominating the high ground and firing from behind cover, the French force poured a deadly fire into the packed British ranks. As the ranks of the British force were thinned by a steady and deadly fire that was coming from an enemy that no one could see, the British regulars lost their steadiness and eventually succumbed to an uncontrollable panic. "And when we endeavoured to rally them," recounted George Washington, then a young officer assigned to Braddock's staff, "it was with as much success as if we had attempted to stop the wild bears of the mountains."

The cost of the debacle was enormous. The French casualties amounted to 23 killed and 16 wounded. The British, however, suffered approximately 977 killed or wounded, including 60 out of 86 officers. Braddock, who had several horses shot out from under him, was killed in the battle.

CHAPTER 3

THE ANGLO-AMERICANS STRIKE BACK

The effectiveness of the French-Canadian and Native strategies for controlling the forests of North America was not lost on the Anglo-American military commanders. "I am ashamed," confided one British colonel, "that they [French] have succeeded in all their scouting parties and that we never have any success in ours." The British command was flying blind, with no intelligence on French preparations or plans. As a result, they were continually surprised and defeated.

Something had to be done! Major-General William Shirley, the commander-in-chief of British military forces in North America, wrote,

> It is absolutely necessary for his Majesty's Service that one Company at least of Rangers should be constantly employed in different Parties upon Lake George and Lake Iroquois [Lake Ontario], and the Wood Creek and Lands adjacent … to make Discoveries of the proper Routes for our own Troops, procure Intelligence of the Enemy's Strength and Motions, destroy their [French] out Magazines and Settlements, pick up small

Parties of their Battoes upon the Lakes, and keep them under continual Alarm.

Major-General Wolfe also thought that the British needed a ranger force that would have a fighting style similar to the French Canadians and Natives. Wolfe insisted, "Our troops must be employed in a very different manner … [they] must learn to live in the Woods as the Natives do — to keep them in a continual apprehension of being attacked and to acquire a perfect knowledge of the Lakes & Rivers, & Hunting Grounds of the Savages."

The English definitely needed to strike back, and rangers seemed like the best way to do that, but how to form a ranger force? The answer came in the form of a charismatic and bold former smuggler, who would quickly galvanize the

Rogers' Rangers were, in essence, the British response to the effective French employment of Canadians and Natives in the scouting and raiding role.

Courtesy Fort William Henry Corporation.

English ranger concept. Robert Rogers was initially a captain of "Company One" of the New Hampshire Regiment. At first, Rogers and his men escorted supply wagons between Albany and Fort Edward. However, Rogers' knowledge and experience with the "haunts and passes of the enemy and the Native method of fighting" soon brought him to the attention of his superior, Major-General William Johnson. By the fall of 1755, Rogers was conducting dangerous scout missions deep behind French lines.

Rogers' efforts soon earned him an overwhelming reputation. "Captain Rogers whose bravery and veracity stands very clear in my opinion and of all who know him," wrote a senior British officer, "is the most active man in our Army." By the winter of 1756, Rogers' bold forays behind enemy lines with his small band of unofficial rangers were regularly reported in newspapers throughout the colonies. They were a tonic to the beleaguered English frontier settlements. Rogers became a propaganda tool to boost morale and his exploits became legendary.

DID YOU KNOW?

Major Robert Rogers

Robert Rogers is one of the legendary colonial heroes from the French and Indian War. Born in Methuen, Massachusetts, on November 18, 1731, Rogers moved to New Hampshire, near present-day Concord, with his family in 1739. He spent his youth exploring the wilderness. His hometown was close to the frontier, making him familiar with Natives and their ruthless raids in time of war.

At the age of only 14 he served in the militia during the War of the Austrian Succession. From 1743–55, some historians suggest that Rogers was a smuggler. In April 1754, he signed up 50 recruits and became a captain of "Company One" of the New Hampshire Regiment. At first, Rogers and his men escorted supply wagons between Albany and Fort Edward. However, Rogers' knowledge and experience with the "haunts and passes of the enemy and the Indian method of fighting" soon brought him to the attention of his superior, Major-General William Johnson. By the fall of 1755, Rogers was conducting scouts behind enemy lines. By the winter of 1756, his bold forays behind enemy French lines were regularly reported in newspapers throughout the colonies. In March 1756, Major-General Shirley, commander-in-chief of the British forces in North America, ordered Rogers to raise a 60-man

> independent Ranger company that was separate from both the provincial and regular units. This company was unofficially called Rogers' Rangers. They were paid and fed by the king, but they were not part of the regular army. They enjoyed more freedom, less military discipline, and higher pay than the regulars, but they did not have the permanency of regular units. A ranger received two shillings and sixpence New York currency per day. This was more than double the wage received by a British soldier.

In March 1756, Major-General Shirley ordered Rogers to raise a 60-man independent ranger company that was separate from both the provincial and regular units. It was named His Majesty's Independent Company (later Companies) of American Rangers. Rogers' unit was directed to scout and gain intelligence in the Lake Champlain area, as well as "distress the French and their allies by sacking, burning and destroying their houses, barns, barracks, canoes, battoes … to way-lay, attack, and destroying their convoys of provisions by land and water."

SHOCKING REALITY

Propaganda

"Propaganda" is the term used for information that is provided with the aim of influencing the beliefs and attitudes of a targeted audience toward a certain cause or position. Propaganda does NOT attempt to provide objective or impartial information. Often, propaganda presents selective facts that can skew perspective or it provides loaded messages that produce emotional instead of rational reactions. Propaganda deliberately attempts to influence attitudes, emotions, opinions, and the actions of individuals for ideological, political, or commercial purposes. In the end, propaganda is designed to change the attitude and support of a target audience toward a particular cause or political agenda.

KEY FACTS

Goreham's Rangers

The success of the French-Canadian raiders forced the British to develop a similar force of their own. One of the first efforts was in 1744, in North America, as part of the larger War of the Austrian Succession (1740–48). During this conflict, the British in the Maritimes were prey to the Abenakis and Micmac war parties that were aligned with the French. As a result, an "independent corps of rangers," also known as the corps of Nova Scotia Rangers, was raised in New England. Two companies were recruited and deployed to Annapolis, Nova Scotia, in July 1744 to reinforce the garrison.

In September, a third company arrived led by Captain John Goreham. Goreham's command was composed of 60 Mohawk and Métis warriors. Familiar with the Native way of war, they swiftly engaged the French and their Native allies. Massachusetts governor William Shirley commended Goreham and his Rangers for their success, stating that "the garrison is now entirely free from alarms." The majority of the companies later returned to Massachusetts, where they originated, leaving Captain Goreham and his company to patrol Nova Scotia alone from 1746–48. Their success was so great that Shirley wrote, "The great service which Lieut. Colonel Gorham's Company of Rangers has been to the Garrison at Annapolis Royal is a demonstration of the Usefulness of such a Corps."

Goreham's Rangers continued to serve on the volatile frontier. Prior to the onset of the French and Indian War, also known as the Seven Years' War (1756–63), Goreham's Rangers were used to protect the British settlements in Nova Scotia against Native raids. However, with the official outbreak of the war they became increasingly involved in military operations because of their expertise at irregular warfare. In 1758, they played an important part in the capture of the strategic Fortress of Louisbourg and a year later assisted in the expedition against Quebec. In fact, at the end of the conflict the British high command rated Goreham's Rangers, although rarely mentioned, as the most highly rated Ranger organization during the war.

British commanders soon called for another 10 companies of rangers to be established. These companies were expected to maintain the lines of communications between towns and advanced forts, procure intelligence, as well as surprise and cut off the enemy's convoys. The rangers were also tasked with "harass[ing] the enemy in Canada by scouting parties in every way they can." In fact, Rogers' commission specifically mentioned the need for a "number of men employed in obtaining intelligence of the strength, situation, and motions of the enemy, as well as other services, for which Rangers, or men acquainted with the woods, only are fit."

The reputation and accomplishments of the rangers soon had an impact on British officers. They all wanted rangers to accompany their expeditions as protection against the enemy. The regular army also valued the rangers' ability to navigate and survive the merciless wilderness. In the course of the war, the rangers participated in virtually every campaign. Lord Loudoun went so far as to consider turning two companies of every regiment of a thousand men into ranging companies. Some British officers, such as George Augustus Viscount Howe and Lieutenant-Colonel Thomas Gage, agreed. They recommended regular light infantry units as a permanent part of the British Army.

Undeniably, Rogers' Rangers, as they became known, brought to life the ranger tradition in North America, which has endured ever since. Their deeds and prowess have with time become legendary. Rogers' Rangers, led by the very adventurous, courageous, and exceptionally tough Robert Rogers, created a very romantic image that seemed to both symbolize and define the strength

LAC, C-20756.

of the American ranger: an adventurous, if not daring, attitude that was overly aggressive and always offensively minded. The ranger tradition also represented individualism and a kind of rebellion against military traditions. Rangers became known as men who were adaptable, robust, and unconventional, both in how they think and how they fight. But above all else, the ranger tradition captured the frontier spirit, if not myth, of the independent fearless fighter with an eagle eye and steady aim, who was at home in the woods and could not be beat in bush combat.

In the end, the rangers filled an important void. Since the British had no Native allies, the rangers were their only hope to gain control of the forests in North America.

The European way of war, which the Natives described as, "In a heap together [so] that it was as easy to hit them, as to hit a house."

69

DID YOU KNOW?

"Ranger"

The term "Ranger" originated in England as far back as the 13th century. It was used to describe far-ranging foresters or borderers, as well as keepers of the royal forest. By the 1600s, the term was also used to refer to unique irregular military organizations, such as the "Border Rangers," who policed the troubled frontier region between England and Scotland. The concept migrated to the New World as well. As early as 1622, faced with conflict against hostile Natives, towns, villages, and isolated plantations and stockades employed bold adventurous armed men to "range" the countryside for signs of enemy activity, as well as possible targets of opportunity. These individuals also escorted surveyors and hunted down escaped slaves. By 1648, a list of conditions by which "raingers and scouts" should be regulated was drawn up by the General Assembly of Maryland.

In the early years of the war, it seemed that only the Rangers were able to strike back at the enemy. This created a great deal of notoriety for the Rangers as Major Robert Rogers was good at providing colourful exploits to raise the morale of the terrorized population along the frontier.

Courtesy Fort William Henry Corporation.

KEY FACTS

The Native View of White Man's War-Making

The Natives found the white man's way of war perplexing and foolish. One Native veteran observed, "Instead of stealing upon each other, and taking every advantage to kill the enemy and save their own people, as we do, they [whites] marched out, in open daylight, and fight, regardless of the number of warriors they may lose!" He added, "After the battle is over, they retire to feast, and drink wine, as if nothing had happened." From the Native perspective, the supreme victory was that which was won with the fewest friendly casualties. For the Native combatants, once individual warriors had proven their martial prowess by taking prisoners, scalps, or plunder — which also had a significant economic benefit — the Natives ended the campaign before they pushed their luck.

In 1756, the Royal Americans, 60th Foot, were organized as light infantry to provide the British with a means of contending with the French Canadians and their Native allies. The regiment was supposed to combine the qualities of the scout with the discipline of the trained soldier. Uniforms and tactics were adjusted to the reality of the wilderness of North America. Musket barrels were painted blue or brown to make them less obvious, a process called "take off the glittering." Military commanders directed that the coats of the light infantry were to be quite plain with the advice that "the less they are seen in the Woods the better." The regular line regiments wore bright red coats with lace, which made the stand out in the forest. One of the Highland Regiments actually traded their kilts for breeches and many officers gave up wearing gorgets (a small piece of armour that goes over the throat) and sashes, which marked them as officers and, therefore, targets for the French-Canadian and Native marksmen. Some officers even went to such extremes as to wear the same tunic as those worn by private soldiers.

KEY FACTS

Robert Rogers' "Rules or Plan of Discipline"

I.   All Rangers are to be subject to the rules and articles of war; to appear at roll-call every evening on their own parade, equipped, each with a firelock, sixty rounds of powder and ball, and a hatchet, at which time an officer from each company is to inspect the same, to see they are in order, so as to be ready on any emergency to march at a minute's warning; and before they are dismissed the necessary guards are to be draughted, and scouts for the next day appointed.

II.   Whenever you are ordered out to the enemies forts or frontiers for discoveries, if your number be small, march in single filed, keeping at such a distance from each other as to prevent one shot from killing two men, sending one man, or more, forward, and the like on each side, at the distance of twenty yards from the main body, if the ground you march over will admit of it, to give the signal to the officer of the approach of an enemy, and of their number, & c.

III.   If you march over marshes or soft ground change your position, and march abreast of each other to prevent the enemy from tracking you (as they would do if you marched in a single file) till you get over such ground, and then resume your former order, and march till it is quite dark before you encamp, which do, if possible, on a piece of ground that may afford your centries the advantage of seeing or hearing the enemy some considerable distance, keeping one half of your whole party awake alternately through the night.

IV.   Some time before you come to the place you would reconnoitre, make a stand, and send one or two men in whom you can confide, to look out the best ground for making your observations.

V.   If you have the good fortune to take any prisoners, keep them separate, till they are examined, and in your return take a different route from that in which you went out, that you may the better discover any party in your rear, and have an opportunity, if their strength be superior to yours to alter your course, or disperse, as circumstances may require.

VI.   If you march in a large body of three or four hundred, with a design to attack the enemy, divide your party into three columns, each headed by a proper officer, and let those columns march in single files, the columns to the right and left keeping at twenty yards distance or more from that of the center, if the ground will admit, and let proper guards be kept in the front and rear, and suitable flanking parties at a due distance as before directed, with orders to halt on all eminences, to take a view of the surrounding ground, to prevent your being ambuscaded, and to notify the approach or retreat of the enemy, that proper dispositions may be made for attacking, defending, & c. And if the enemy approach in your front on level ground form a front of your three columns or main body with the advanced guard, keeping out your flanking parties, as if you were marching under the command of trusty officers, to prevent the enemy from pressing hard on either of your wings, or surrounding you, which is the usual method of the savages, if their number will admit of it, and be careful likewise to support and strengthen your rear-guard.

VII.   If you are obliged to receive the enemy's fire, fall, or squat down, till it is over, then rise and discharge at them. If their main body is equal to yours, extend yourself occasionally; but if superior, be careful to support and strengthen your flanking parties, to make them equal to theirs, that if possible you may repulse them to their main body, in which case push upon them with the greatest resolution with equal force in each flank and in the center, observing to keep at a due distance from each other, and advance from tree to tree with one half of the party before the other ten or twelve yards. If the enemy push upon you, let your front fire and fall down, and then let your rear advance thro' them and do the like, by which time those who before were in front will be ready to discharge again, and repeat the same alternately, as occasion shall require; by this means you will keep up such a constant fire, that the enemy will not be able easily to break your order, or gain your ground.

VIII.   If you oblige the enemy to retreat, be careful, in your pursuit of them, to keep out your flanking parties, and prevent them from gaining eminences, or rising grounds, in which case they would perhaps be able to rally and repulse you in turn.

IX.   If you are obliged to retreat, let the front of your whole party fire and fall back, till the rear hath done the same, making for the best ground you can; by this means you will oblige the enemy to pursue you, if they do it at all, in the face of a constant fire.

X.   If the enemy is so superior that you are in danger of being surrounded by them, let the whole body disperse, and every one take a different road to the place of rendezvous appointed for that evening, which must every morning be altered and fixed for the evening ensuing, in order to bring the whole party, or as many of them as possible, together after any separation that may happen in the day; but if you should happen to be actually surrounded, form yourselves into a square, or if in the woods, a circle is best, and if possible, make a stand till the darkness of the night favours your escape.

XI.   If your rear is attacked, the main body and flankers must face about to the right and left, as occasion shall require, and form themselves to oppose the enemy, as before directed; and the same method must be observed, if attacked in either of your flanks, by which means you will always make a rear of one of your flank-guards.

XII.   In general, when pushed upon by the enemy, reserve your fire till they approach very near, which will then put them into the greatest surprize and consternation, and give you an opportunity of rushing upon them with your hatchets and cutlasses to the better advantage.

XIV.   When you encamp at night, fix your centries in such a manner as not to be relieved from main body till morning, profound secrecy and silence being often of the last importance in these cases. Each centry therefore should consist of six men, two of whom must be constantly alert, and when relieved by their fellows, it should be done without noise; and in case those on duty see or hear anything, which alarms them, they are not to speak, but one of them is silently to retreat, and acquaint the commanding officer thereof, that proper disposi-tions may be made; and all occasional centries should be fixed in like manner.

XV.   At the first dawn of day, awake your whole detachment; that being the time when the savages chuse to fall upon their enemies, you should by all means be in readiness to receive them.

XVI.   If the enemy should be discovered by your detachments in the morning, and their numbers are superior to yours, and a victory doubtful, you should not attack them till the evening, as then they will not know your numbers, and if you are repulsed, your retreat will be favoured by the darkness of the night.

XVII.   Before you leave your encampment, send out small parties to scout round it, to see if there be any appearance or track of an enemy that might have been near you during the night.

XVIII.   When you stop for refreshment, chuse some spring or rivulet if you can, and dispose your party so as not to be surprised, posting proper guards and centries at a due distance, and let a small party waylay the path you came in, lest the enemy should be pursuing.

XIX.   If, in your return, you have to cross rivers, avoid the usual fords as much as possible, lest the enemy should have discovered, and be there expecting you.

XX.   If you have to pass by lakes, keep at some distance from the edge of the water, lest, in case of an ambuscade or an attack from the enemy, when in that situation, your retreat should be cut off.

XXI.   If the enemy pursue your rear, take a circle till you come to your own tracks, and there form an ambush to receive them, and give them the first fire.

XXII.   When you return from a scout, and come near our forts, avoid the usual roads, and avenues thereto, lest the enemy should have headed you and lay in ambush to receive you, when almost exhausted with fatigues.

XXIII. When you pursue any party that has been near our forts or encampments, follow not directly in their tracks, lest they should be discovered by their rear-guards, who, at such a time, would be most alert; but endeavour, by a different route, to head and meet them in some narrow pass, or lay in ambush to receive them when and where they least expect it.

XXIV. If you are to embark in canoes, battoes, or otherwise, by water, chuse the evening for the time of our embarkation, as you will then have the whole night before you, to pass undiscovered by any parties of the enemy, on hills, or other places, which command a prospect of the lake or river you are upon.

XXV. In padling or rowing, give orders that the boat or canoe next the sternmost, wait for her, and the third for the second, and the fourth for the third, and so on, to prevent separation, and that you may be ready to assist each other on any of emergency.

XXVI. Appoint one man in each boat to look out for fires, on the adjacent shores, from the numbers and size of which you may form some judgement of the number that kindled them, and whether you are able to attack them or not.

XXVII. If you find the enemy encamped near the banks of a river or lake, which you imagine they will attempt to cross for their security upon being attacked, leave a detachment of your party on the opposite shore to receive them, while, with the remainder, you surprize them, having them between you and the lake or river.

XXVIII. If you cannot satisfy yourself as to the enemy's number and strength, from their fire, & c. conceal our boats at some distance, and ascertain their number by a reconnoitring party, when they embark, or march, in the morning, marking the course they steer, &c. When you may pursue, ambush, and attack them, or let them pas, as prudence shall direct you. In general, however, that you may not be discovered by the enemy on the lakes and rivers at a great distance, it is safest to lay by, with your boats and party concealed all day, without noise or shew, and to pursue your intended route by night; and whether you go by land or water, give out parole and countersigns, in order to know one another in the dark, and likewise appoint a stations for every man to repair to, in case of any accident that may separate you.

Courtesy Fort William Henry Corporation.

A Ranger in winter dress.

The change in philosophy also showed in how the Europeans adapted their tactics. Rangers and scouts were always included in the advance party of any moving force. Major-General Wolfe instructed all detachments and outposts to strengthen their camps by either digging trenches around them or palisades (wooden stakes placed in a close row like a fence). Sentries were never to be placed in musket-range of woods unless they were hidden behind rocks or trees, and he cautioned his commanders never to stop, camp, or pass through openings without first examining the area for a potential ambush or subsequent attack.

DID YOU KNOW?

How to Fight an Indian

A veteran Indian fighter watched some British regulars doing drill one day. When the British soldiers were finished, he spoke to the officer in charge and told him, "We exercised our men that were to fight against the French and Indians, in a different manner."

The British captain replied, "Pray, sir, how is that?"

The Indian fighter answered, "Only to load quick, hit the mark, that is our whole exercise."

The captain was astounded. "What!" he said, "Do you take aim at the enemy?"

"Yes, good aim, or not fire," responded the veteran Indian fighter, "you will scarce find upon attack six Indians together, and you must divide yourselves in small parties everywhere to oppose the scattered enemy."

The captain, still unconvinced, ended the discussion by asking, "Do you think when a body of regulars keep rank and fire regular platoons that an irregular attack can defeat them? It cannot be, Sir, you're certainly mistaken."

The French soon noticed a difference. Major-General Montcalm, the commander-in-chief of the French military forces in North America, noted in his journal (July 1757) that "the enemy is very alert and they continually have scouts in the field." He attributed the lack of success of his scouting and raiding detachments to the English efforts. Montcalm called Major Robert Rogers the "famous partisan" and considered Rogers' Rangers to be "elite troops." Colonel Bougainville made similar observations around the same time. He noted the enemy was always alert and constantly had scouting parties out to patrol the wilderness.

And so the stage was set for the final showdown. The French, English, and their colonial allies all had specialized forces that could deal with the savage wilderness of North America. What quickly followed was a deadly game of cat and mouse between the Anglo-American rangers and the French-Canadian and Native raiders.

KEY FACTS

"Standing Orders of Rogers' Rangers"

A modernized abbreviated version captures a rustic charm and pragmatism that is used to help modern-day soldiers with patrolling. However, they are a modern creation and are not the original rules set by Rogers. Nonetheless, they have been posted on the United States Rangers website. The "Standing Orders of Rogers' Rangers" are given as:

1. Don't forget nothing.

2. Have your musket clean as a whistle, hatchet scoured, sixty rounds powder and ball, and be ready to march at a minute's warning.

3. When you're on the march, act the way you would if you was sneaking up on a deer. See the enemy first.

4. Tell the truth about what you see and what you do. There is an army depending on us for correct information. You can lie all you please when you tell other folks about the Rangers, but don't ever lie to a Ranger or officer.

5. Don't never take a chance you don't have to.

6. When we're on the march we march single file, far enough apart so one shot can't go through two men.

7. If we strike swamps, or soft ground, we spread out abreast, so it's hard to track us.

8. When we march, we keep moving till dark, so as to give the enemy the least possible chance at us.

9. When we camp, half the party stays awake while the other half sleeps.

10. If we take prisoners, we keep'em separate till we have had time to examine them, so they can't cook up a story between'em.

11. Don't ever march home the same way. Take a different route so you won't be ambushed.

12. No matter whether we travel in big parties or little ones, each party has to keep a scout 20 yards ahead, 20 yards on each flank, and 20 yards in the rear so the main body can't be surprised and wiped out.

13. Every night you'll be told where to meet if surrounded by a superior force.

14. Don't sit down to eat without posting sentries.

15. Don't sleep beyond dawn. Dawn's when the French and Indians attack.

16. Don't cross a river by a regular ford.

17. If somebody's trailing you, make a circle, come back onto your own tracks, and ambush the folks that aim to ambush you.

18. Don't stand up when the enemy's coming against you. Kneel down, lie down, hide behind a tree.

19. Let the enemy come till he's almost close enough to touch, then let him have it and jump out and finish him up with your hatchet.

CHAPTER 4

A DEADLY GAME OF CAT AND MOUSE

Many historians have called Lake Champlain and the Richelieu River Valley a North American invasion corridor. The Richelieu River connects Lake Champlain to the St. Lawrence River, which runs through New France, past Montreal and Quebec, and on to the northern parts of the British colonies. So a potential invader would need access to this "water highway" in order to attack their enemy.

Both the French and the English built up their defences in their territories. The French built Fort Chambly, Fort St. Frédéric, and Fort Ticonderoga at strategic points along the waterway to control access and to prevent an enemy from moving north to attack New France. The British built Fort William Henry on the shore of Lake George and Fort Edward farther inland to stop any attackers from moving south into the British Colonies. This strategically important terrain became known as the Lake Champlain theatre of operations. It also became a deadly battleground.

Since the waterways were the most efficient means of moving large numbers of troops and equipment to launch an attack, both sides were actively scouting and patrolling in an effort to discover what the enemy was planning, and, if possible, to launch attacks that would destroy and disrupt enemy plans. Not surprisingly, it became contested ground for the French-Canadian raiders and Rogers' Rangers.

SHOCKING REALITY

Fort William Henry Massacre

Fort William Henry was the northernmost British outpost on the southern end of Lake George in New York State. It was built in September 1755, under the orders of Sir William Johnson following the Battle of Lake George. As the battle was inconclusive, he decided to construct fortifications near the site of battle. The French withdrew and began to build Fort Ticonderoga near the northern end of the lake.

Fort William Henry was named after Prince William, the younger son of King George II, and Prince William Henry, a grandson of the king. Its main purpose was to act as a staging post for an eventual attack against the French at Fort Ticonderoga and Fort St. Frédéric. For that reason, it was a strategic location on the frontier between the English colonies and New France. The fort itself was made of wood with bastions on the corners. Its walls were 9.1 metres thick, with log facings around an earth filling. A dry moat surrounded three sides of the fort. The fourth side sloped down to the lake itself. Access to the fort was limited to a bridge across the moat. Within the fort were two-storey-high wooden barracks, a magazine, and a hospital. The fort could house approximately 400 to 500 men. Additional troops were housed in an entrenched camp about 700 metres southeast of the fort.

In late July 1757, Lieutenant-Colonel George Munro, the commander of Fort William Henry, learned that the French were planning to attack. He received reinforcements and his command swelled to 2,300 troops, who began to prepare to defend the fort and surrounding fortifications. However, conditions in the fort were poor and there was an outbreak of smallpox. As expected, Montcalm and his attacking force of 8,000, which consisted of 3,000 regular soldiers, 3,000 militia, and 2,000 Natives, arrived on August 3 and began siege operations and bombarding the fort immediately. After several days, the British had suffered hundreds of casualties and lost a number of their heavy cannons and mortars. In addition, the fort walls were breached in a number of locations. With no hope of reinforcement, Munro surrendered on August 9, 1757, to very generous terms. Munro would be allowed to march out of the fort with colours flying and his troops would be allowed to keep their weapons and officers their baggage. However, all British personnel were not to engage in the war for 18 months and all French prisoners captured since 1754 were to be released within three months.

The following morning the British garrison formed up to march south to Fort Edward, 22 kilometres away. As they were making their preparations, Natives entered the fort and surrounding buildings and killed and scalped wounded British soldiers who were unable to make the march. They also began to loot stores from the buildings, swarming the column and snatching weapons, clothing, and individuals. Those who resisted were killed or dragged away. As the column began to march away, the Natives attacked its rear elements. Montcalm and other French officers attempted to stop their allies, but with limited success. Under constant attack, the column disintegrated as individuals attempted to escape. In the end, British casualties have been estimated at approximately 200. However, the Natives suffered from their actions as well. They killed and scalped sick and wounded individuals, as well as dug up graves of those who died to retrieve scalps. They took clothing and blankets from the British. Many of those items, as well as scalps, were infected with smallpox, a disease to which the Natives had no immunity. As a result, the disease cut a swath of death through numerous Native villages.

In the end, the event strained relations between Montcalm and his Native allies. It also enraged the British, who held Montcalm and the French responsible for the atrocities that had been committed, since Montcalm had promised Munro protection. As a result, when the French capitulated at Montreal, in 1760, the British refused to grant them the honours of war, specifically the right to keep their regimental colours, because of the events at Fort William Henry.

During the French and Indian War there were countless patrols, close calls, and skirmishes between both sides. There were a number of epic combats between the French-Canadian partisans and Rogers' Rangers that are worth retelling. The following provides an account of three savage battles of survival that capture the essence of the combat experienced in the forests of the Lake Champlain theatre of operations during the war.

On January 15, 1757, Major Robert Rogers set off from Fort Edward on a scout with a force of 53 hand-picked, experienced woodsmen. They stopped at Fort William Henry where they prepared supplies and made snowshoes while they waited for reinforcements. Two days later they were joined by Captain Speakman and 16 of his men, as well as Ensign James Rogers and 14 men from Captain Hobbs' Ranger Company. Everyone was issued rations for two weeks (dried beef, sugar, rice and dried peas, and cornmeal, which was held in a knapsack that was slung over the shoulder, and diluted rum in their canteen). They also carried 60 rounds of ammunition (ball and powder) and blankets that they draped over their heads and fastened to their waist belts.

SHOCKING REALITY

Smallpox

Smallpox is a deadly infectious disease unique to humans. It is believed to have emerged about 10,000 BC, and by the end of the 1700s was estimated to have killed approximately 400,000 Europeans per year. Of those who were infected, 30 to 60 percent, and 80 percent of all children, died from the disease. The disease is highly contagious, transmitted through the inhalation of airborne variola virus, usually droplets emitted from oral, nasal, or bodily fluids from an infected person or through contaminated objects such as bedding or clothing. Infected people develop a rash and high fever.

Smallpox made its debut in North America in Plymouth, Massachusetts, in 1633, with devastating effect on the Natives and native-born colonists. During the Pontiac Uprising, in 1763, the British at Fort Pitt intentionally passed two blankets and a handkerchief that had been exposed to smallpox to representatives of the attacking Native tribes in order to spread the disease in an attempt to end the siege of the fort.

The last naturally contracted case of smallpox occurred on October 26, 1977, when an unvaccinated hospital cook in Somalia was infected. The World Health Organization officially declared smallpox eradicated in 1980.

On January 17, just as the sun began to slip behind the horizon, Rogers' force set off on their mission. Their task was to gain intelligence on the French garrison, specifically their strength and intentions. Key to their mission was also to cause as much mayhem and alarm behind French lines as possible in order to disrupt, harass, and destroy enemy forces, equipment, and morale.

Rogers chose to travel on the ice of Lake George to avoid the rugged, mountainous terrain around the Lake George/Lake Champlain corridor. Travelling in single file, they made good time despite bad weather, and stopped for the night in no man's land. The next morning Rogers discovered that 11 men had been injured by the strenuous march. He immediately sent them back to Fort William Henry. His war party was now only 74-men strong.

DID YOU KNOW?

Langy

Jean-Baptiste Levrault de Langis Montgeron (known as "Langy" in English) was considered the ideal French-Canadian leader, who allowed New France to defy the odds as long as it did.

Langy was born in 1723 and followed in the footsteps of his father and three older brothers by serving in the colonial regular troops. He began his military career on Cape Breton Island, and in 1755, as an ensign, participated in the unsuccessful defence of Fort Beauséjour. During this campaign his superiors identified him as "an extraordinarily brave officer."

Langy became a key player on the Lake Champlain–Lake George front. He was continually raiding, scouting, and gathering intelligence. His forays took him deep into enemy territory, where his attacks left the British unnerved and consistently on the defensive. The information Langy brought back on enemy fortifications and/or their intentions (drawn from prisoners) kept the French well informed. Throughout the spring of 1758, Langy was constantly in the field attempting to determine the English intentions. Although seizing many prisoners, no useful information was discovered. Then, in June, Langy captured 17 Rangers, who revealed an impending attack against the strategic Fort Ticonderoga. On July 4, Montcalm, demonstrating his confidence in the Canadian partisan leader, trusted Langy "to go observe the location, number, and the movements of the enemy." Langy's force departed and returned the following night with news that the British invasion force was en route. As a result, Montcalm ordered his troops to take up defensive positions.

However, Langy's job was not finished. He deployed once again to monitor the British advance. On July 7 he had a chance encounter with the British advance guard. In the bloody clash that followed, both sides suffered substantial casualties. Langy's men killed Brigadier Lord Howe during the skirmish. With his death the British suffered a critical loss of leadership that doomed their attack. Although outnumbered almost four to one, Montcalm went on to route Major-General James Abercromby's army.

As the tide of the war changed, Langy remained instrumental in harassing the English forces, particularly the British Rangers who had begun burning homesteads of *les habitants* during the siege of Quebec City. He also crossed swords with Major Rogers on two more occasions. On the first, he discovered whaleboats that were used by Rogers and 142 Rangers for their raid on the Abenaki village of St. Francis. The subsequent pursuit ended with 69 Rangers dead or captured and the others narrowly escaping with their lives. The second encounter was even more successful. Despite the fall of Quebec in September 1759, Langy, operating from Îsle aux Noir (near Montreal), continued his aggressive raids. In February 1760, as Rogers was en route to Crown Point from Albany, his convoy of sleds was ambushed by Langy. Recognizing Rogers in the first sled, Langy focused his attack there. The initial volley killed the horses and Langy's force pounced on Rogers and his 16 recruits. In the ensuing melee, Rogers and seven others escaped to Crown Point. The other nine Rangers were killed or captured. Langy also seized 32 brand-new muskets, 100 hatchets, 55 pairs of moccasins, and £3,961 — the payroll for the troops at Crown Point.

His final raid was conducted six weeks later, once again near Crown Point. Representative of his skill and daring, Langy was able to capture two British regular officers, a Ranger officer, and six troops, without a firing shot. His luck, however, had run out. Shortly after his return to Montreal with his prisoners, Langy drowned while trying to cross the St. Lawrence River in a canoe. Captain Pierre Pouchot noted the news in his journal, commenting that Langy was "the best leader among the colonial troops." An English newspaper also reflected that assessment, "Mons. Longee, a famous partisan, fell through the ice sometime and was drowned … his loss is greatly lamented by all Canada, and his equal is not to be found in that country."

They continued down the lake, hugging the shoreline to avoid detection. As Rogers neared the French lines he decided it was too dangerous to stay in the open and led his group off the ice. Strapping on snowshoes, they took to the thick forest. Progress was slow as they trudged through the deep snow and forced their way through the pines. By January 20, Rogers was well behind enemy lines.

The Rangers woke the following morning to a steady downpour. They dried their muskets under covered fires in pits dug out of the snow, about three feet deep. Then they set off, changing course and stealthily marching due east under the dripping trees until they reached the ice of Lake Champlain. They were now approximately halfway between the French strongholds of Fort Ticonderoga and Fort St. Frédéric. Amazingly, as the Rangers stepped out of the forest, a French convoy of sleighs that had just departed Fort Ticonderoga and were heading to Fort St. Frédéric to pick up supplies, appeared in the distance.

Rogers immediately deployed his men to ambush the French. He ordered Lieutenant Stark and 20 of his men to cut off the lead sled, while Rogers and another group backtracked to act as a block if the sleighs tried to retreat. He left Captain Speakman in the middle with the rest of the war party. As Rogers hurried to get into position he suddenly realized there were 8 to 10 more sleds than they had at first realized! Rogers tried to send word to Stark to stay hidden, but it was too late.

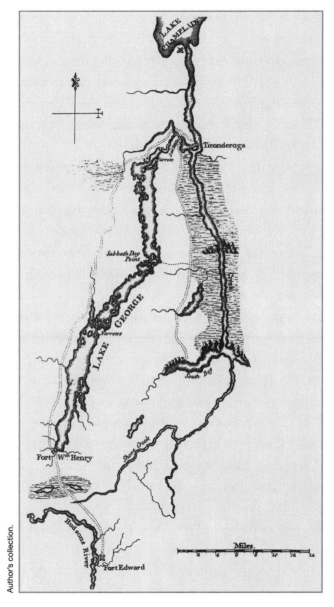

Author's collection.

The Lake George/Lake Champlain theatre of operations.

The first sled was quickly engaged as Stark and his men ran from the trees across the slippery snow to intercept it. After that there was no turning back. Rogers reacted instantly and led his group into the fray. In fact, he captured the first prisoner as the lead sleigh tried to avoid Stark's men. Despite the frantic efforts of the Rangers, the rear sleds careened wildly away, racing back to the safety of Fort Ticonderoga. Pursuit was hopeless. In total, the Rangers captured three sleds, six horses, and seven prisoners.

The problem was that Rogers and his men were deep behind enemy lines and the French knew they were there and would be looking for them. Making the situation worse, Rogers learned from his prisoners that 200 Canadians and 45 Natives, all experienced in wilderness warfare, had just arrived at Fort Ticonderoga. Fifty more Natives were also expected from Fort St. Frédéric any day. Plus there were already 600 French regular troops at Fort St. Frédéric and 350 at Fort Ticonderoga.

The mission had become a race for survival. Rogers wasted no time. He ordered his group to assemble and quickly marched them through the wet pines to his camp from the previous night. Meanwhile, back at Fort Ticonderoga, the alarm was raised. The French commandant of the fort immediately sent out approximately 100 regular soldiers and colonial troops under the command of Captain Basserode. The commandant was also fortunate enough to have with him the experienced ensign of *les Compagnies Franches de la Marine*, Charles de Langlade, who led about 90 Natives and Canadian volunteers. Together they hoped to catch the English as they returned to Fort William Henry.

As the Rangers dried their muskets, Rogers assembled his officers. Although many disagreed with Rogers' decision to retrace their steps, he overruled them and ordered them to prepare their soldiers for the march. As the rain continued to fall, the Rangers, with their muskets and powder carefully tucked under the blankets they wore as overcoats, set out in single file.

Painting, "Triumphant Return," by Robert Griffing, Paramount Press.

Langlade quickly figured out the route Rogers would take. The rugged, inhospitable terrain narrowed the options of approach and passage through the Adirondack Mountains. Langlade had guessed correctly. He soon found the path the Rangers had taken. The French followed the trail until they found a good place to ambush the British. The constant rain and wetness made their weapons unreliable, so they had to find a spot where they could quickly attack and overwhelm the English interlopers.

At mid-afternoon, as the front of the English party reached the top of the west side of yet another ravine, the sudden roar of a musket discharging was quickly drowned out by a thunderclap of explosions as the nearly 200 Frenchmen, Canadians, and Natives deployed in a semicircle around the valley,

A Native war party returns to its village with plunder taken during the massacre at Fort William Henry.

unleashed their fire on the unsuspecting Rangers. Luckily, the volley was not very effective due to the wetness of the muskets. However, the French, who were between 5 and 30 yards from the Ranger column, fell upon them with tomahawks and bayonets.

SHOCKING REALITY

Captured! The Account of Major Putnam

For some, the battle of survival continued beyond the savage fight in the choking alders and forests near Fort Sainte-Anne. Major Putnam was such an individual. He was at the front of the column when the ambush was triggered, and discharged his musket immediately. However, unable to reload, without support, and confronted by the enemy, Putnam quickly surrendered. He was unceremoniously tied to a tree while his captors fought the remainder of Putnam's column. During the course of the battle, Putnam found himself in the line of fire — musket balls were whistling through the air close to his body. Some thudded into the tree to which he was tied.

The musket balls were not his only concern. Behind the enemy's skirmish line, Putnam became the centre of attention on a number of occasions. First, a young warrior took time from the battle to test Putnam's nerve, or his own accuracy, or perhaps both. Repeatedly, the Native threw his tomahawk attempting to get as close to Putnam as possible without actually hitting him. Putnam barely escaped harm on a number of throws. Next, he had to deal with a French officer who attempted to discharge his musket into his chest. Fortunately, the weapon misfired, and, deaf to Putnam's pleas for quarter, the Frenchman butt-stroked Putnam across the jaw.

As the momentum of the battle began to swing in favour of the British, some Natives untied Putnam and dragged him along as they withdrew. A short distance away from the battlefield, the Natives stopped and stripped Putnam of his belongings. He lost his coat, vest, stockings, and shoes. Then he was loaded with as many of the packs of the wounded as could be piled upon him. Strongly pinioned and with his wrists tied as closely and tightly as possible, so that he could be led by a cord, he was marched off into the wilderness at a quick pace.

Putnam's agony is not hard to imagine. His hands swelled from the tightness of his ligature, causing him great pain. His bare feet, ripped and torn from the hard terrain and brush, bled. Exhausted, in pain, and succumbing to the weight thrust upon him, Putnam deplored the Natives to just kill and scalp him now and get it done with it. A French officer intervened and ordered his hands untied and some of the weight removed. However, his relief was only temporary.

As the march continued, Putnam was continuously abused. At one point a deep wound was inflicted on his cheek with a tomahawk. Worse yet, upon reaching the site where the French would encamp for the night, Putnam recoiled in horror as he realized what was about to happen. The Natives stripped him naked and tied him to a tree. Enraged by the day's events and their lost comrades, the Natives had decided to roast Putnam alive. As the rope bit into his flesh, he could feel the rough bark of the tree dig into his back. To the accompaniment of high-pitched screams, the Natives piled dry brush and sticks in small piles at a short distant from Putnam, then they set the piles alight.

A sudden downpour doused the flames, but the Natives were not going to be cheated. They quickly nursed the piles of kindling until a fierce fire raged. Putnam soon felt the scorching heat and he squirmed his body from side to side in a futile attempt to avoid it. His discomfort and impending doom fuelled the excitement of his torturers.

> Putnam had resigned himself to his fate when a sudden commotion caught his attention. A French-Canadian officer, who turned out to be none other than Marin himself, bullied his way through the crowd and kicked the burning piles aside. He then untied Putnam and reprimanded Putnam's tormentors. Marin stayed with Putnam until he could be handed over to the Native who had actually taken him prisoner. The worst was over.
>
> Putnam was returned to Fort Ticonderoga, where he was interviewed by Major-General the Marquis de Montcalm and then escorted to Montreal by a French officer who "treated him with the greatest indulgence and humanity."

Despite their obvious disadvantage, the Rangers reacted quickly. The opening volley killed two and wounded several others, including Rogers, but instinct, as well as an ingrained sense of survival, took over. Rogers, known for his courage and coolness under fire, ordered his men to return fire and withdraw to the ridge on the far side. Lieutenant Stark and Sergeant Brewer saw the crisis unfolding and immediately formed up the rear of the column (approximately 40 men) into a defensive posture on the high ground and prepared to cover the retreat of their comrades.

The struggle was desperate. The Rangers closest to the front became embroiled in savage hand-to-hand combat. Not all could break away — those who did were chased and only reached the safety of the far hill because of the brisk fire from Stark's group that beat back the French pursuers. But not before several of the Rangers were killed or taken captive.

Rogers deployed his remaining force. Lieutenants Stark and Baker held the centre. Ensign Rogers and Sergeants Walter and Phillips were moved into a position in reserve to watch the enemy's movement and prevent the Rangers from being flanked. Both sides continued to exchange fire. Darkness was now the Rangers' only hope. The Rangers were outnumbered, several were

Drawing by Ted Zuber.

wounded, and they were low on ammunition — they were in a precarious position. And to make things worse, Rogers was unsure if French reinforcements were closing in on them.

The French and Canadians tenaciously pressed the attack all afternoon. The Rangers repeatedly beat them back with a steady, accurate fire. The battle

French-Canadian partisans and their Native allies ambush British soldiers.

97

eventually settled into an exchange of shots. Rogers suffered his second wound when he took a musket ball through his wrist, leaving him unable to load his musket. Fearing this would have a negative impact on morale, Rogers sent word to his officers that he was fine and that all should keep up a diligent fire and hold their positions.

As the woods echoed with the clap of constant musket fire, darkness started to seep into the already overcast sky. As the light finally disappeared, both sides stopped firing. The cloak of darkness could not have come soon enough. Many of the Rangers were severely wounded and could not travel without help, and their ammunition was almost exhausted. Moreover, their proximity to Fort Ticonderoga gave the enemy a distinct advantage. They could easily deploy more forces and simply overwhelm the hard-pressed Rangers during the night, or at first light. To avoid that, Rogers decided to use the night to make his escape. He issued his orders and the men who could still march set off.

The French stayed on the battlefield throughout the night, attempting to track down the Rangers. For the seriously wounded, the night brought no safety. The ones who had withdrawn to the rear of the position and built a small fire to keep warm suddenly realized they could no longer see or hear any of their men. The grim reality was that the Rangers capable of withdrawing had escaped, leaving the wounded at the mercy of the Natives.

The next morning, the Rangers who had managed to escape the French noose reached Lake George, approximately six miles south of the French pickets. Once they were there, Rogers dispatched Lieutenant Stark with two men to Fort William Henry to arrange sleigh transport for the wounded. On January 23, 1757, a party of 15 Rangers and a sled met the ragged surviving column on the ice. That night the survivors, 45 effective and nine wounded, arrived at Fort William Henry.

The grim, bitter wilderness struggle was very costly. The Rangers suffered 14 killed, six wounded, and six captured — a total of 26 out of 74 participants, or a casualty rate of 35 percent. French accounts revealed their losses to be 14 killed and 24 wounded.

The next major engagement did not turn out any better for the Rangers. On March 10, 1758, Major Robert Rogers left Fort Edward with 180 men. The force cautiously crept up the shore of Lake George. The lake was still frozen but free of snow, so the Rangers used ice-creepers to move north toward the French lines. As the Rangers neared enemy territory they slept during the day and marched in the dark of night. By March 13, they left the ice of the lake and moved into the forests. They cached their rucksacks and sleds and took only their fighting order. Rogers decided to ambush a French patrol as it left their defensive lines. He picked the terrain for the ambush carefully and then divided his force in two. Now it was a matter of waiting.

Rogers had his men hide behind trees overlooking a ravine with a frozen stream. A French column of approximately 100 men, led by Natives, worked its way down the ice of the stream bed, which was easier to travel on than the deep snow. As the head of the French column drew even with Rogers' left flank, Rogers fired his musket as a signal to attack. The woods suddenly filled with a continuous clap of thunder as the Ranger line fired into the French, Canadians, and Natives. It was as if a scythe cut through their ranks. As the survivors tried to escape, Rogers' right flank rushed down into the ravine to cut them off. It seemed like the Rangers had bested their enemy.

Suddenly, another wave of thunder reverberated through the winter wilderness. Rogers realized immediately that he had just attacked the vanguard of a larger force. The hunter became the hunted. The Rangers that rushed into the ravine now found themselves overwhelmed and fighting for their lives to escape back up the hill to friendly lines. The Rangers fought from tree to tree and tried to create a defensive perimeter. The Canadians and Natives darted from cover to cover, attempting to infiltrate and cut off the Rangers.

The French attacked relentlessly. The Rangers, realizing their lives were at stake, were able to throw back the assaults. But they could not last forever. Ninety minutes after the first shot was fired, as darkness began to fall, the French succeeded in collapsing the centre of Rogers' position. Rogers and 20 men fell back on their depth position. They fired a volley and then scattered into the darkness to make their individual escapes.

To speed up his getaway, Rogers threw off his jacket, which held his commissioning scroll. As a result, a rumour that Rogers was killed at the Battle of the Snowshoes circulated in the French camp. It was not, however, true. Rogers had made a narrow escape. Of the 181 individuals who began the expedition, only 54 survived and made it back to Fort Edward. Once again, Rogers had been bested by the French Canadians.

Less than six months later, the two forces would meet once again in a bitter showdown. This time it was the French Canadians who found themselves trapped behind enemy lines. The morning began like many others for Captain Joseph Marin, the veteran French-Canadian partisan leader who was preparing his war party for the next leg of their raid. A sudden musket shot shattered the morning stillness of the Adirondack wilderness. Within seconds two more shots rang out. As they echoed through the forest, Marin realized that the enemy was very close. He quickly and quietly deployed 500 Canadians, coureurs de bois, and Natives into a crescent-shaped ambush on the edge of the forest clearing. Within minutes, his large force practically vanished as they melted into the thick brush, awaiting the arrival of the British-American force that was apparently close by.

Marin and his raiding party had been on their way to strike the English at Fort Edward. They were emboldened by the French victory at Fort Ticonderoga a month earlier, on July 8, 1758, when Montcalm's force of 3,600 men defeated Major-General James Abercromby's army of 15,000. In its aftermath, the Canadians and their Native allies mounted a number of raids. In fact, just days earlier on July 28, another French Canadian, La Corne, with 300 Canadians and Natives, massacred a convoy of 116 men and women between Fort Edward and Halfway Brook. Upon hearing of the outrage, Major-General Abercromby immediately ordered Majors Robert Rogers and Israel Putnam, with a combined force of 1,400 men, to hunt down La Corne. Despite their haste they reached the narrow of Lake Champlain too late; La Corne narrowly missed their noose. However, the stage was now set for yet another encounter between Marin and his nemesis Rogers.

DID YOU KNOW?

Marin

Joseph Marin de La Malgue (known as Marin) was another legendary French-Canadian partisan leader who struck terror into the English settlements. He was born in Montreal in 1719, into a family steeped in martial tradition. His grandfather was an officer in the colonial regular troops and his father, Paul Marin de la Malgue, was also an officer of the colonial regular troops who became renowned for his diplomatic, trading, and fighting skills. Marin the elder, at the age of 30, took command of Chagouamigon (near present-day Ashland in northern Wisconsin on Lake Superior). This appointment carried the customary monopoly of the region's fur trade, but his primary responsibility was to ensure and maintain the alliance between the Native nations and France.

The young Marin was a famous partisan leader in his own right. From an early age he was brought up on stories and the reality of fighting in the wilderness of North America. His father, who was greatly feared and respected by the Natives, taught the younger Marin his trade. In 1732, at only 13 years old, Marin's father sent him to explore the *Pays-d'en-Haut*, which refers to the northwest (i.e., the upper Great Lakes basin). For the next 13 years, as a cadet in the colonial regular troops, he stayed in that area. This experience was critical in his development, providing him with an understanding of the complexities of the fur trade. More importantly, he became skilled at wilderness travel, and knowledgeable about Native culture and temperament. In fact, he became fluent in Sioux and several Algonquin dialects. He also gained military experience during the campaign against the Chickasaws in 1739–40, and he earned his diplomatic spurs when he made peace and trade agreements with the Sioux west of Baie-des-Puants (present-day Green Bay, Wisconsin).

In 1745, Marin and his father were recalled to the east to fight in the war in Acadia and Cape Breton Island. Although his influence was minimal at the time, this latest exposure to war provided more experience. Later that year, Marin, under his father's command, participated in a large-scale raid against the English, which devastated Schuylerville and neighbouring areas in New York. During the next two years, 1746–48, Marin was busy in Acadia, Grand-Pré, Cape Breton Island, and the New York frontier, learning and plying the deadly craft of *la petite guerre*. He was promoted to the rank of second ensign at the end of the conflict in 1748.

The following year, the governor of New France, La Jonquière, gave Marin command of the post at Chagouamigon. Marin found himself in his father's old job. He was also assigned the responsibility of making peace with the Sioux and Ojibwas who were locked in conflict with each other, as well as the French. He succeeded.

In 1750, Marin was promoted full ensign. He was recalled to Montreal on July 11, 1756, with a large contingent of Native warriors. Later that summer, he participated in the successful campaign to capture the British fort at Oswego, where he and his Menominee warriors continually beat larger British forces.

In August, Marin led a force of approximately 100 on a raid against Fort William Henry on Lake George, New York, and defeated a force of about the same size as his own. His constant raids, particularly because of the brutality and savage nature of the French Canadians and Natives, terrorized both the garrisons of the frontier forts and the settlements at large. In December 1756, Marin led a force of 500 French Canadians and Natives on another raid that tore a path of destruction through New York. Six months later, in July 1757, Marin led a small reconnaissance party to the vicinity of Fort Edward in New York. His force crept up close to the fort and then annihilated a 10-man patrol, and then a 50-man guard. Finally, totally overwhelmed by British reinforcements, he expertly held them off for an hour and then withdrew. In total, the action cost him only three men.

The next major battle took place in August 1758. It pitted Marin against his arch-nemesis, Major Robert Rogers. Rogers and the British force of about 530 men were careless, and Marin and his raiding party figured out that they were outnumbered. Marin quickly deployed his Canadians and Natives and skilfully sprung an ambush that caught the enemy completely by surprise. Although inflicting heavy casualties and capturing several prisoners, the remainder of the British force reacted well and the battle soon settled into a bitter war of attrition. Marin was caught behind enemy lines, between a large force and an even larger pool of reinforcements who were only hours away. So he broke his command up into small groups and they melted away.

In January 1759, Marin was promoted to captain. He spent the first part of the year conducting raids against the frontier settlements in Pennsylvania and Maryland. That summer he joined a relief effort to raise the British siege of Fort Niagara (near present-day Youngstown, New York). However, his force was ambushed and he was taken prisoner. Not surprisingly, his capture was announced as a great triumph in the English colonies.

Three days later, 11 Rangers patrolling the Wood Creek approach from Fort Ticonderoga stumbled upon fresh tracks of a large Native war party. They followed the trail for four miles, then decided to stop for a meal. In an instant the tables were turned. The Rangers were surrounded by 50 Natives — they attacked and the hunter became the prey. In the desperate and savage struggle that followed, eight Rangers and 17 Natives were killed, and two Rangers were captured. Only one Ranger, Sergeant Hackett, escaped. As he fled to Fort Edward he discovered the tracks of an even larger enemy war party, apparently heading in the direction of Fort Edward.

When Hackett reached Fort Edward he reported what he had seen to Abercromby, who devised a plan to intercept and destroy the unidentified French raiding party. Abercromby sent a dispatch to Rogers and Putnam, who were still in the field, to take 700 chosen men and 10 days of provisions and "sweep all that back country" of South Bay and Wood Creek to Fort Edward in hopes of finding the French-Canadian war party.

On the night of July 31, Rogers, Putnam, and their force camped on Sloop Island. The next day was spent preparing the expedition and on August 2, Rogers and Putnam left with separate groups to set ambushes where the Wood Creek meets East Bay and South Bay. Unfortunately, no one stumbled into either of the traps. Four days later, Rogers and Putnam rejoined forces and marched to the decaying ruins of Fort Sainte-Anne, where they camped on the night of August 7, 1758.

Up until that point, the Rangers hadn't accomplished much. Other than the near capture of an enemy canoe with six warriors, there was no sign of enemy forces. The men were becoming bored and distracted. One hundred seventy soldiers were released and they returned to Fort Edward. Rogers had just 530 men remaining when they settled in for the night.

The next morning, as the sun began to rise over the hills, Rogers and Putnam prepared for the march west to Fort Edward. For some reason, Rogers, who had literally written the book on light infantry warfare in North America, "Standing Orders of Rogers' Rangers," had a lethal lapse of judgment. He and Ensign William Irwin, of Gage's Light Infantry Regiment, had a friendly argument about who was the more skilled marksman. Things quickly got a whole lot less friendly, and words soon led to action: the two began firing at targets to prove who was the better shot.

Little did they know that the enemy was in the area. As the shots echoed through the forest, the French-Canadian commander, Captain Marin, who was close by, reacted instantly. His trained eye surveyed the ground and he quickly spotted an ideal ambush site. He developed a plan and swiftly deployed his forces. Between the two forces lay a clearing that was choked with alder and brush, cut in half by a single narrow trail that led directly into the forest where Marin had positioned his men. The dense cover would allow the enemy to unwittingly walk right into Marin's ambush location. By the time they realized the threat it would be too late.

Major Putnam led the column. He had his 300 Connecticut Provincials leading. Behind him followed Captain James Dalyell with detachments of British infantry from the 80th and 44th Regiments. Rogers brought up the rear with his Rangers and the remaining Provincials. Putnam marched right into the ambush. Lieutenant Tracy and three soldiers were suddenly overwhelmed and dragged into the thick brush. Then the French Canadians and their Native allies unleashed a lethal volley on the unsuspecting English troops caught in the open clearing. "The enemy rose as a cloud and fired upon us," recorded one participant, "the tomahawks and bullets flying around my ears like hailstones."

Putnam immediately ordered his men to return fire and a deadly melee began in the thick alder brush and forest, but the odds were against them. "The enemy discovering them," recounted Dr. Caleb Rea, "ambushed'm in form of a Semi Circle which gave the Enemy a great advantage of our men." The provincial troops quickly broke and fell back behind the regulars, who were led forward by Captain Dalyell.

Photo by Silvia Pecota.

A most deadly weapon — the tomahawk.

The battle became centred around a huge fallen tree. Marin pounded the British with four volleys of fire before the "Red Coats" managed to flank the tree and engage the enemy in hand-to-hand combat. At this point, the momentum of the battle began to turn in favour of the British. Major Rogers was at the back of the column with his men. He quickly moved his forces to the sound of battle. The antagonists were then evenly matched and the action raged on for another hour.

The thick bush and alder at the edge of the forest turned the battle into a series of very personal fights, as the small area prevented much group action. At one point, a monstrous Native chief, who stood six feet four inches tall, jumped upon the large fallen tree and killed two British regulars who tried to oppose him. A British officer, who was trying to help the fallen soldiers, hit the giant with his musket. Although he drew blood, he only enraged the Native, who was about to dispatch the officer with his tomahawk when Major Rogers proved his marksmanship and shot the Native chief dead.

Marin tried to outflank the British by turning their right flank. He made four valiant attempts, however, Rogers and his Rangers gave no ground. As the fight raged around him, Rogers sensed the flow of battle and reversed the initiative. He began to shift his Rangers right in a bid to out-manoeuvre the French Canadians. Some Canadians began to break. Then the Rangers charged. Half the Rangers would fire, while the other half would reload. That way, they kept up a constant fire and forward movement. Under this constant fire and pressure, the remainder of the French Canadians gave way.

However, Marin was no novice in bush warfare. Realizing the situation, he avoided a rout and destruction of his force by dividing his surviving force into small parties and taking different withdrawal routes. The groups reunited later that night and made camp in a secluded location surrounded by impenetrable swamp.

The British chose not to pursue the French. Instead, they stayed on the battlefield and buried their dead. As always, the casualty figures vary, however, it appears that British-American losses added up to 53 killed, 50 wounded, and four taken prisoner. The French Canadians suffered approximately 77 killed.

Once the dead were buried, Rogers and his party continued their march to Fort Edward, carrying their wounded on litters made of strong branches with blankets strung over them. En route, a relief force of 400 soldiers under Major Munster, which included an additional 40 Rangers and a surgeon, met the column. Rogers then encamped for the night. The latest desperate fight combat had no overall effect on the struggle for North America. What the combatants in the depth of the Adirondack wilderness did not yet know was that the strategic tide of the war had begun to shift. Soon, the focus of operations would be farther north.

Drawing by Ted Zuber.

Hand-to-hand combat.

CHAPTER 5

THE BEGINNING OF THE END

Lake Champlain was an important battleground in the struggle for the North American wilderness, but it was just one piece of the larger war. Importantly, the emphasis placed on the struggle for control of the forests was about to change. Lieutenant-General Louis-Joseph de Montcalm-Gozon, Marquis de Montcalm was the commander-in-chief of all French regular forces in New France. He reported to the Canadian-born Governor Vaudreuil, which was difficult for Montcalm since he had an utter contempt for the governor, the Canadians, the Natives, and the Canadian way of war.

Montcalm was a vain, opinionated, and stubborn officer with a quick temper. He believed that the Canadians were an undisciplined rabble of little to no military value. "The Canadians thought they were making war when they went on raids resembling hunting parties," quipped Montcalm. This feeling was shared by his French officers. Colonel Bougainville wrote with disdain in his journal: "To leave Montreal with a party, to go through the woods, to take a few scalps, to return at full speed once the blow was struck, that is what they [French Canadians and Natives] called war."

LAC, C-27665.

Lieutenant-General Louis-Joseph de Montcalm-Gozon, Marquis de Montcalm.

DID YOU KNOW?

Lieutenant-General Louis-Joseph de Montcalm-Gozon, Marquis de Montcalm

The Marquis de Montcalm was born to a noble family on February 28, 1712. He entered the military at 17 and saw military service during the War of the Polish Succession and the War of the Austrian Succession, where his distinguished service earned him a promotion to brigadier-general. In 1746, during the Battle of Piacenza, he was captured after receiving five sabre wounds while rallying his men. After several months of imprisonment he was released and was later able to return to active service as a result of prisoner exchanges.

He joined the Italian campaign in 1747, and was again wounded, this time by a musket ball. When that war ended the following year, and with the commencement of yet another conflict in North America, Montcalm was sent to Canada following the capture of Major-General Baron Jean-Armand Dieskau at the Battle of Lake George on September 8, 1755. Montcalm, now promoted to major-general, arrived on May 13, 1756. He reported to the governor and was responsible only for the discipline, administration, and internal ordering of the six French regular army battalions. He was strictly the commander in the field and had to obey all orders from the governor. However, after his stunning victory at Fort Ticonderoga, on October 20, 1758, he was promoted to lieutenant-general, the second highest rank in the French Army. He outranked the governor of New France and commanded all military forces in the colony.

Finally, he was able to implement his strategy, which concentrated on the defence of Quebec City, in a European-style battle. He felt that a large invasion force would not be able to get up the St. Lawrence River and expected the attack to come from the south. When he learned that an invasion flotilla was on its way upriver, he heavily fortified Quebec and the northern shore of the river. After the invaders tried unsuccessfully to land several times, the British were finally able to get approximately 4,500 men on the Plains of Abraham. Montcalm decided to leave the city's defences and meet the British troops on the field of battle. His forces were defeated and during the withdrawal he was hit in the abdomen by a musket ball. He died the next day, on September 14, 1759.

Montcalm and his officers constantly criticized Vaudreuil's strategy and methods. Quite simply, the Canadian way of war was repugnant to them. Montcalm's long-rooted experience and belief in the European model of warfare caused him to complain constantly about the French-Canadian "petty means" and "petty ideas." He placed absolutely no value in the taking of "a few scalps and burning a few houses." Montcalm knew that the Canadian methods could not inflict a lasting defeat on the English. He was convinced that the only hope lay in a strong defence in one location. He believed that spreading the few soldiers they had among the distant and remote forts and outposts on the fringes of New France was a waste of resources. Montcalm insisted that the only way to save New France was to concentrate as many of its military forces as possible at the critical point, which he believed was Quebec City.

The difference of opinion between Vaudreuil and Montcalm on how best to fight the war could not have been greater. The differing views on strategy were made even worse by the petty jealousy over authority and the desire for recognition and reward. Not helping at all was the fact that Vaudreuil was Canadian-born and Montcalm was French. Because he was the governor, Vaudreuil was the senior officer. He had the authority to insist that his strategy of defending forts and outposts on the fringes of New France and an active raiding program be maintained. Vaudreuil was adamant that they contest all of the "ground on our frontiers inch by inch with the enemy."

Photo by Author.

The guns of Fort Ticonderoga guard the approach to Lake Champlain.

Vaudreuil had learned through hard experience that aggressive offensive action would be the only practical defence for New France. "The Marquis de Montcalm," wrote an exasperated Vaudreuil in 1758, "is not ignorant that superiority of numbers being on their side, I dare not promise myself any success unless I can surprise them by an attack in the inclement season."

Vaudreuil's approach was logical and had been successful in the past. The traditional policy also allowed him to use the troops at his disposal to their best advantage. He concluded that the Canadians and colonial troops of La Marine "knew how to make bloody war on the British, while Montcalm's

Courtesy Fort William Henry Corporation.

A French regular soldier of the Royal Roussillon Regiment.

French regulars fought in too gentle a manner." Equally important, Vaudreuil understood that the Canadians and their Native allies did not operate with the same confidence under the command of the regular French Army as they did under the control of their own Canadian officers.

SHOCKING REALITY

The Raid on St. Francis

In August 1759, two British regular officers who were travelling under a purported flag of truce were captured by a group of St. Francis Natives. When Major-General Jeffery Amherst, the new commander-in-chief of British forces in North America, found out, he became outraged. He then ordered Major Robert Rogers to take a force of 220 men and wipe out the village at St. Francis. However, between Rogers and the village lay 240 kilometres of uncharted wilderness. Moreover, the French still controlled that part of Lake Champlain.

Rogers and his force left Crown Point in the dead of night on September 13. Ten days later, after eluding French naval patrols, they hid their boats and moved inland for the final approach. However, two days later, two Natives who were left behind to guard their hidden whale boats caught up to Rogers and warned him that the French had found the boats and were on his trail. After a gruelling trek through impenetrable forest and spruce bogs, Rogers and his now-depleted force (due to injury and sickness) reached their objective. Just before dawn, on October 6, they struck the unsuspecting Native village. The attack was completely unexpected. Many people were killed before they could fully realize what was happening. Some tried to run for the river but were cut down by Rangers who had been posted there to stop any escape. By 7:00 a.m., it was all over. The entire town was torched. Rogers suffered one dead and one seriously wounded. He estimated the Native losses at 200 to 300.

However, his ordeal was not yet over. The raiding party still had to make it back to friendly lines. For eight days they marched through harsh terrain and freezing wind-driven rain. Food began to run out and exhaustion set in. Rogers decided to break the force up into smaller parties so it would be easier to hunt to feed the now starving Rangers. Some of the groups were attacked by the pursuing Natives and killed or captured.

Rogers' party eventually made it to the designated rendezvous point at Wells River, but the relief party that was supposed to be there with supplies had left. All Rogers found was a smoking fire. He had to trek to the closest outpost, Post No. 4. Finally, on October 31, Rogers made it to friendly lines. He immediately sent out rescue parties with provisions to bring in the remainder of his raiding party. Throughout the early days of November, Rangers would straggle in. In the end, Rogers lost 49 men. All but two of those captured by the Natives were killed.

The struggle between the two French senior appointments continued until fate decided for them. Montcalm's stunning victory at Fort Ticonderoga, at the tip of Lake Champlain, in July 1758, was the catalyst for dramatic change. The French forces under Montcalm were outnumbered almost four to one. With only 3,600 troops, mostly French regulars, Montcalm decisively beat the attacking British Army of approximately 15,000 troops, consisting of 6,000 regulars and 9,000 provincials. Under the command of Major-General James Abercromby, the assaulting Anglo army was the largest force ever assembled in North America at that time. Hunkered down behind a wall of earth and logs, Montcalm's troops fought back the relentless English assaults. By day's end, the English Army was in full flight back to Fort William Henry. The British suffered 1,944 casualties; 1,610 of those were regulars. The French suffered only 377 casualties. One of Montcalm's senior officers, Brigadier-General François-Gaston Chevalier de Lévis, jubilantly wrote, "This brilliant victory saved Canada." By stopping the

English at the head of Lake Champlain, they had blocked the water highway to Quebec. Once again, any English hope of launching an invasion against New France was thwarted in the distant backwaters of the wilderness.

KEY FACTS

The Battle of Ticonderoga

The Battle of Ticonderoga was fought on July 8, 1758, about one kilometre from Fort Ticonderoga itself. The French force of approximately 4,000 men, under Major-General Montcalm, dug entrenchments on high sloping ground on the approach to the fort, which Montcalm felt would be easier to defend. His opponent, Major-General James Abercromby, had a force of 17,000 men, the largest seen in North America at that time.

Abercromby was confident that he would win with such a large force. He launched frontal assaults against the French trenches, without artillery since he did not want to wait for it to be dragged forward. The attack began at noon. The British launched no fewer than six assaults against the entrenchments. All the attacking British troops could see was the end of the hats and musket barrels of the French.

By seven o'clock that night the British soldiers finally gave up and withdrew to their landing place. Many of the troops were completely demoralized and continued the withdrawal back to Fort William Henry. The French defenders were exhausted and did not pursue the retreating British forces. They cleaned their muskets and slept in the entrenchments, expecting another series of attacks in the morning. On July 10, not having seen any sign of movement from the British, Montcalm sent out a reconnaissance party, which confirmed that Abercromby's army had disappeared. The French had won a decisive victory. Historians estimate that the British suffered approximately 2,500 casualties, the French 377.

LAC, C-4664.

A contemporary, albeit inaccurate, depiction of the Battle of Ticonderoga.

The victory gave Montcalm his opportunity. He used this latest success, which was achieved without the assistance of Canadians or Natives, to make his point to the French king that a concentration of force in the heart of the colony was the best strategy to defeat the British. In the fall of 1758, he sent Colonel Bougainville to Paris with a letter explaining the situation in New France. The French government was in disarray and already sceptical of the regime in New France. Not surprisingly, particularly after such a convincing victory at Ticonderoga, Montcalm was promoted to lieutenant-general. This promotion meant that he outranked Governor Vaudreuil. Montcalm was now in command of all military forces in Canada, which included the French Canadians and Natives.

SHOCKING REALITY

"Ravenous Hell Hounds"

The Natives developed a fierce reputation among both the white soldiers and colonists. They earned a feared reputation as marksmen and experts in wilderness warfare. These tactical skills, combined with their brutality and cruelty, soon paralyzed their opponents. The mere presence of Natives, or the sound of their war cry, created panic in the ranks. The "ravenous hell hounds," as the Natives were often called by their European counterparts, terrified their foes. "The yells of our Natives," wrote Montcalm to his mother, "promptly decided them [English garrison at Oswego]. They yielded themselves prisoners of war to the number of 1,700, including eighty officers and two regiments from England."

Vaudreuil recounted the same story. "The cries, threats, and hideous howlings of our Canadians and Natives," he boasted, "made the enemy quickly decide."

At the prelude to the attack on Fort William Henry, the ambush of a resupply flotilla met with the same fate. "Terrified by the sight of these Monsters [Natives], their agility, their firing, and their yells," recalled Bougainville, "they [British] surrendered almost without resistance."

The mere thought of battling the savages unsettled both the British regulars and the American militia. "The men from what stories they had heard of the Natives in regard to their scalping and tomahawking," wrote a British officer in his journal, "were so panic struck that their officers had little or no command over them." George Washington recounted an escort from Winchester to Fort Cumberland. At the first firing from the Natives, he stated, the men broke and ran back to Winchester, with less than half the force even stopping to fire a shot. One British official wrote to the prime minister, "We have seen that our regulars do not fight well in woods, the yell [of the Natives] is horrid to their ears, and soon throws them into confusion."

Equally important, Montcalm's strategy of pulling back from the frontier forts and outposts to concentrate on the defence of Quebec was accepted by the government of France. The French ministers of war and the marine hoped that Montcalm could deliver an encore performance of his victory at Ticonderoga — only this time they hoped he could do it at the gates of Quebec City.

EPILOGUE

The new French approach completely changed the war. Montcalm had rejected the Canadian way of war. He did not want to fight in the wilderness, he wanted a battle fought between regular armies. He would soon get his wish. Politics across the ocean would play a dramatic part in changing the course of the war. British Prime Minister William Pitt decided that North America would be his primary focus for the Seven Years' War. His intent was to conquer New France once and for all. He had the Royal Navy blockade its shores, and he dispatched the largest English army North America had seen at that time.

With his massive regular military forces, reinforced with American militia troops, Pitt undertook a three-pronged strategy to invade New France. In the west, Pitt tasked Brigadier John Forbes to capture Fort Duquesne in the Ohio Valley. After a long campaign where the British suffered numerous setbacks, the French finally abandoned Fort Duquesne in late November 1758. A British force of 2,500 soldiers, sent to launch yet another attack on the fort, arrived just in time to watch the French forces blow it to pieces. The British promptly moved in and began to rebuild it as Fort Pitt.

The second, or centre prong, of Pitt's three-pronged invasion of New France was Major-General Abercromby's failed attack on Fort Ticonderoga, or Fort Carillon, as the French called it.

SHOCKING REALITY

The Burning of the North Shore

Major-General Wolfe's invasion force landed on the Île d'Orléans in late June and began siege operations. Wolfe became increasingly frustrated with his inability to engage the main French army and destroy them. On several occasions Montcalm had frustrated his attempts at landing troops or decisively engaging the French forces. Moreover, Canadians and Natives continually harassed his forces. In some cases, Canadians, and even priests, stripped down and dressed as Natives during the guerilla war they waged against the invading British force.

On Wolfe's arrival in June, he invited the *habitants* to return to their homes, but warned them that if they took up arms against the British they would suffer dire consequences. Late in July, he issued another warning based on the attacks his forces were suffering and gave the Canadians a final ultimatum. On August 4, he unleashed his troops and a vicious campaign of terror began. Wolfe's light infantry, Rangers, and regular troops burned entire villages and imprisoned *habitants* to punish them for their active participation, as well as to goad Montcalm into leaving his entrenchments and bring his forces into the open to fight. On August 22, Wolfe wrote, "I intend to burn all the country from Camarasca to the Point of Levy." By mid-September 1759, parishes on both sides of the St. Lawrence resembled a wasteland. Historians estimate that upwards of 1,400 farmhouses were burned to the ground.

The third prong was the attack on the French Fortress of Louisbourg on Cape Breton on the east coast. This strategic fort guarded access to the St. Lawrence River and the supply line to Quebec City. After a siege of almost two months, the French garrison finally surrendered on July 26, 1758. New France was now completely on the defensive.

In 1759, when the British resumed their offensive, the French frontier forts pulled back as soon they came under pressure. Under Montcalm's orders, a small rear party force at each fort and outpost set explosives and destroyed the fortifications as the English force approached. No major battle was offered. The French forces just melted away. Montcalm was finally able to concentrate his forces at Quebec City to prepare for the Anglo-American attack.

Drawing by Ted Zuber.

Members of the Black Watch scale the cliffs leading to the Plains of Abraham.

SHOCKING REALITY

Duplicitous Allies

The competition between the French and the British for the allegiance of the Natives had one specific negative effect for both sides. Neither one of the European powers wanted to offend their presumed allies, so the Natives were given unrestricted access to the camps and forts. The Natives, in turn, used this freedom of movement to spy and report on the preparations and plans of a belligerent to their respective enemy. The information was normally given in exchange for payment and/or to demonstrate allegiance to one side.

French commanders noted in their memoirs that the ambassadors who came to provide information on British preparations had also likely come to conduct a reconnaissance on those of the French. For this reason, Montcalm consciously spread false information and plans among the Natives. Even the governor of New France, Le Marquis de Vaudreuil, who normally praised the Natives, wrote to the Ministry of Marine and conceded that there was no doubt that the Natives spied on their supposed French allies. He said that he reproached them for their treason and warned them of the consequences should they continue.

The British perspective was no different. Major-General Jeffery Amherst, who was appointed the British commander-in-chief in 1759, wrote, "If the Natives know them [operational plans] the French will have it; it is their business to give intelligence to both sides."

In the summer of 1759, the Natives actively conspired with the British to assist with the capture of Fort Niagara. The French officer responsible for the resupply of the fort was intentionally led into an ambush by his Native guides. Although they remained neutral during the initial engagement, once the supply column collapsed the Natives "fell on them like so many Butchers."

Furthermore, Captain Pouchot, the commandant of the fort, was assured by his Native allies that "if we learn that the Englishman is plotting anything against you, we shall inform you immediately, so that you are not taken by surprise." But just over a month later an entire British force passed through the Iroquois territory and appeared without warning before the fortress. To add further insult, once the fort had fallen, the Natives, most well-known to the French garrison, swarmed in to pillage and plunder the contents of the fort, even attempting to strip the French soldiers, their former compatriots, of their arms and possessions.

To alleviate his manpower crisis, since the French king had refused to send any reinforcements, Montcalm also drafted colonial troops and the fittest of the Canadian militia into his regular line battalions. Rather than allow them to fight how they knew best, in the form of *la petite guerre*, he forced them to fight in the European manner. As far as Montcalm was concerned, war in North America would now be fought as he knew it in Europe.

As the British swung to the offensive, bringing their massive advantage in economic, naval, and military power to bear, the last bits of French strength in North America began to wane. The blockade at sea and the loss of the Fortress of Louisbourg starved New France of supplies. Moreover, the destruction of Fort Frontenac and Fort Duquesne in 1758, which represented two of France's most strategic fortifications on the frontiers, was a turning point in the relationship between the Natives and the French. Once the French were unable to provide supplies or presents to their allies, and no longer had the forts that represented power and trading outlets, there was little incentive for the Natives to remain allied with the French. In fact, it became readily apparent to the Natives that the French were losing the war. By August 1759, Montcalm observed that he had few Natives and that the French and Canadians were almost completely alone.

And so, with only token or no resistance at all from French forts or outposts to slow down the invading English armies, the French frontier quickly collapsed to Quebec City, the very heart of New France. More significant was the British control of the St. Lawrence River. The French, who had believed the St. Lawrence was too difficult to navigate for a full fleet of ships, were surprised when an invasion flotilla sailed up the river and unloaded approximately 9,000 British troops on June 26, 1759, on the Île d'Orléans.

Montcalm, however, had prepared for the defence of Quebec City. By the end of May 1759, he had 14,000 troops spread along the shores of the St. Lawrence River, waiting to repel the English invaders. Throughout the summer, the British, under command of Major-General James Wolfe, attempted to draw out Montcalm's forces and engage them in battle, but the French remained entrenched in their defences and easily repulsed any English attacks.

With the autumn fast approaching, Wolfe became desperate. By early September, time was running out. The Royal Navy would have to leave soon to avoid being trapped in the ice of the St. Lawrence River. Wolfe knew that if he did not bring the campaign to a decisive end soon, the harsh Canadian winter would. He decided to gamble. On the night of September 12, 1759, the Royal Navy ships sailed underneath the guns of the Fortress of Quebec. Wolfe landed his force at the base of a cliff at L'Anse-au-Foulon. At the landing site was a small trail that cut up through the rugged cliffs, leading to a large field known as the Plains of Abraham, located to the west of the city's walls.

DID YOU KNOW?

Major-General James Wolfe

Major-General James Wolfe was born on January 2, 1727. He was the son of Lieutenant-General Edward Wolfe, a respected British officer-general. Major-General Wolfe received his commission at a young age. He saw extensive service in Europe, where he fought in the War of the Austrian Succession and the suppression of the Jacobite Rebellion.

During the Seven Years' War, Wolfe increased his military reputation. His participation in the campaign at Rochefort in 1757 boosted his career, and he was promoted to colonel shortly after. In January 1758 he was given the rank of brigadier in America and was appointed as one of the brigade commanders for the expedition to capture the strategic French Fortress of Louisbourg on Cape Breton Island. There he led a daring landing that enabled the British to gain a foothold and begin the siege. Throughout the operation Wolfe demonstrated himself to be a very effective and energetic officer.

Following the capture of Louisbourg, Wolfe returned to London, England. On January 12, 1759, he was appointed commander-in-chief of the land forces for the expedition against Quebec and given the rank of major-general. He was given 10 battalions of regular infantry, approximately 8,500 well-trained soldiers. However, by that time Wolfe was in poor health, which added to some of the problems that he experienced. Despite this, his invasion force landed on the Île d'Orléans on June 27. For the next two months, Wolfe unsuccessfully tried to bring Montcalm's army to battle. The summer began to slip away and the admiral of the British fleet warned Wolfe that he must soon set sail so that his ships would not be caught in the ice of the St. Lawrence River. Finally, on the night of September 12, 1759, Wolfe gambled on a daring plan. He landed his soldiers at the Anse-au-Foulon, where under cover of night they scaled the cliffs leading to a farmer's field that was known as the Plains of Abraham. Wolfe formed up his regulars and awaited the French attack. He allowed Montcalm's force to approach and then opened up with a deadly volley that threw the French ranks into confusion. Then the British line charged and threw the French and Canadian soldiers into complete rout. However, Wolfe was mortally wounded. At first he was struck in the hand or wrist, which he ignored. But, as he led the right wing in pursuit of the French he was hit again in the body by a musket ball. He died shortly afterward. His body was taken back to England and he was buried in the family vault at Greenwich.

LAC, C-73720.

Montcalm rallying his troops to battle.

Throughout the night, Wolfe's soldiers scrambled up the narrow trail and cliff. Amazingly, by the early morning hours of September 13, Wolfe had managed to deploy approximately 4,500 troops on the Plains of Abraham. At first, Montcalm thought the landing was a ploy to trick him into abandoning his positions to the east of the city, in Beauport, where a large landing would be easier to accomplish along the flat shoreline. When he finally realized his mistake, Montcalm rashly rushed the troops available to him out onto the plain. He feared that any delay would only serve to strengthen the British.

Montcalm assembled the troops he had gathered in line, in accordance with European custom. He then advanced toward the British lines. Once they were within range, the French began to fire volleys, which were returned by the British. However, the deployment became ragged as Canadians, who had been recently drafted into the regular ranks with little training and a stronger inbred experience with their own way of war, threw themselves to the ground to reload. Others bolted for the cover of trees to join other Canadians sniping from the flanks. The Canadians, who were deployed to swell the ranks of the regulars, were "only suited to petite-guerre … [and they] were a hindrance to the operation," complained Captain Pouchot. He explained that their "little experience of European tactics," especially the British volley, "shook the nerve of the Canadians, who had little experience of being under fire without cover [and] they broke ranks and fled."

Not surprisingly, the Canadians' actions caused disarray and confusion in the French ranks. The final straw came when the entire British line fired in unison, causing a wall of lead to cut a swath through the French ranks. As if the deadly British volley had not been enough, the British forces then gave a resounding battle cry and charged through the cloud of smoke that hung over the battlefield. The sight of British regulars with gleaming bayonets, and kilted Scotsmen with claymores, turned the French confusion into utter panic. The French forces turned on their heels and streamed from the battlefield, hotly pursued by the British.

LAC, C-6491.

A contemporary depiction of the Battle of the Plains of Abraham.

Ironically, it was the Canadians — the very troops who were chastised for their "cowardice" and failure to maintain formation during the initial confrontation — who saved the French regulars from complete annihilation. Fighting as they had always practised, from behind cover as irregular fighters, their courage and marksmanship became an asset. Their continuous fire forced the charging British troops to redirect their focus. Instead of chasing the French regulars from the battlefield, the British had to clear the woods of the Canadians. This relieved pressure for the escape of Montcalm's regulars, albeit at great cost in Canadian blood.

One journal account of the period is telling. The author wrote,

The rout was total only among the regulars; the Canadians accustomed to fall back Native fashion and to turn afterwards on the enemy with more confidence than before, rallied in some places, and under cover of the brushwood, by which they were surrounded, forced diverse [British] corps to give way, but at last were obliged to yield to the superiority of numbers.

KEY FACTS

The Fortress of Louisbourg

Louisbourg was a French fort on the southeast coast of Cape Breton Island. When the fort was first established in 1713, the location was chosen because it dominated the approaches to the Gulf of St. Lawrence. This allowed the fortress to protect Quebec and other French settlements along the river, as well as provide a staging base from which to raid the sea lanes between New England and Britain. In addition, the location provided natural protection. The harbour was well-protected and ice-free so it could be a winter port for French naval forces on the Atlantic seaboard. Moreover, there was a natural reef that created a barrier for ships approaching the fortress and a large island that allowed for a battery of guns to keep invaders away. Louisbourg also became a very important economic centre, becoming the second largest commercial city in New France, after Quebec City. By 1752, the population of Louisbourg was 4,174.

The fortress itself took the French 25 years to complete. The fort was surrounded by four kilometres of walls, which on the western side were 30 feet high and 36 feet across. The fortress city had four bastions and two gates that allowed access. On the eastern side of the fort, 15 guns protected the harbour. The walls at this point were 16 feet high and 6 feet thick. The fortress boasted embrasures for 148 cannons. There was also a fortified island in the harbour. The walls of the island fort were 10 feet high and 8 feet across. Here 31 large cannons were mounted facing the harbour.

The fortress was attacked on two occasions and it fell both times. The first time was during the War of the Austrian Succession, in 1745. A British force from New England, supported by the British Royal Navy, captured the fortress after a six-week siege. However, the fortress was returned to the French as part of the Treaty of Aix-la-Chapelle, which ended the war. The British traded Louisbourg for its trading post at Madras, India, which had been captured by the French. Having given up Louisbourg, the British built their own fortified naval base in Atlantic Canada in 1749, in Chebucto Bay, which they named Halifax. Louisbourg was attacked by the British again in 1758 before the British attack on Quebec City. After a siege of almost two months, the fortress capitulated. The fortress was razed by British engineers in 1760 so that it could never be used again. In 1961, the government of Canada began reconstruction of the fortress as a national historic park.

Despite the bravery of the Canadians, Quebec City surrendered days later. The British maybe have won the capital of New France, but they were surrounded. The French still had large forces in Montreal. In late April 1760, the French, under Marquis de Levis, attacked the British at Sainte-Foy just outside Quebec City. Levis' 8,000 troops fought the British for two hours. The British commander, Major-General James Murray, quickly realized his troops were in danger of being cut off and ordered a withdrawal into the safety of the walled city of Quebec, which they had occupied since the battle the previous September.

By April 29, the French forces were 600 metres from the walls of Quebec City. They started preparing for a siege. It was important that they capture the city before the ice in the St. Lawrence melted, allowing a relieving force to arrive by ship. On May 15, the Royal Navy arrived and the French forces withdrew back to Montreal.

LAC, C-3499.

The Death of Major-General Wolfe.

With the Fortress of Quebec secure, by early summer the British began to move against Montreal, the last key city in New France. The English advanced from Oswego on Lake Ontario in the west; from Quebec City, reinforced with troops from Louisbourg in the east; and up Lake Champlain and the Richelieu River from the south. Slowly, the noose began to tighten around Montreal. With no hope of reinforcement, and with their troops deserting in large numbers, the French surrendered on September 8, 1760. The struggle for the wilderness of North America was over. The British had won.

What is remarkable is that the French, Canadians, and their Native allies had lasted as long as they did. New France had maintained French control over large areas of North American wilderness for more than a century, despite the ever-growing British military and economic power, as well as the exploding Anglo population in the British colonies to the south. The explanation lay in their adherence to the "Canadian way of war," which they practised with such skill and tenacity.

The French and Canadians were aware that they could expect only limited assistance from France. Resources, particularly manpower and defence spending, were always at a premium. As a result, military operations had to be limited. What they could do was largely tactical, often relying on careful use of resources and alliances to achieve an influence greater than what New France's military, economic, or political strength would normally allow. They fought an aggressive war for the wilderness, practising *la petite guerre*. In essence, the battle cries in the wilderness that ensured control of the forests, as well as the raiding that continually disrupted and dislocated the Anglo-American forces to the south, allowed the French, Canadians, and their Native allies, to maintain a military and political stature beyond what should have been possible.

SELECTED READINGS

Alberts, Robert C. *The Most Extraordinary Adventures of Major Robert Stobo.* Boston: Houghton Mifflin Company, 1965.

Bearor, Bob. *The Battle on Snowshoes.* Bowie, MD: Heritage Books Inc., 2005.

Brumwell, Stephen. *Redcoats: British Soldiers and War in the Americas, 1755–63.* Cambridge, U.K.: University of Cambridge, 2002.

Cooper, James Fenimore. *The Last of the Mohicans.* London: Woodsworth Classics, 1993 (1826).

Cuneo, John R. *Robert Rogers of the Rangers.* New York: Oxford University Press, 1959.

Darlington, Mary C., ed. *History of Colonel Henry Bouquet and the Western Frontiers of Pennsylvania 1747–1764.* New York: Arno Press, reprint 1971.

Drimmer, Fredrick, ed. *Captured By the Natives: 15 Firsthand Accounts 1750–1870.* New York: Dover Publications Ltd., 1961.

Hamilton, Charles, ed. *Braddock's Defeat: The Journal of Captain Robert Cholmley's Batman; The Journal of a British Officer; Halkett's Orderly Book.* Norman, OK: University of Oklahoma Press, 1959.

Hamilton, Edward P., ed. *Adventures in the Wilderness: The American Journals of Louis Antoine de Bougainville, 1756–1760.* Norman, OK: University of Oklahoma Press, 1990.

Horn, Bernd. "Hollow of Death: Rogers' Rangers Desperate Fight for Survival, 21 January 1757." *Canadian Military History*, Vol. 14, No. 4, Autumn 2005, 5–15.

_____. "La Petite Guerre: A Strategy of Survival." Bernd Horn, ed. *The Canadian Way of War: Serving the National Interest.* Toronto: Dundurn Press, 2006, 21–56.

_____. "Marin and Langy — Master Practitioners of *la petite guerre.*" Bernd Horn and Roch Legault, eds. *Loyal Service: Perspectives on French-Canadian Military Leaders.* Toronto: Dundurn Press, 2007, 53–86.

_____. "Terror on the Frontier: The Role of the Natives in the Struggle for North America." Bernd Horn, ed. *Forging a Nation: Perspectives on the Canadian Military Experience.* St. Catharines, ON: Vanwell Publishers, 2002, 43–64.

Kopperman, Paul E. *Braddock at the Monongahela.* Pittsburg: University of Pittsburg Press, 1977.

Leckie, Robert. *A Few Acres of Snow: The Saga of the French and Indian Wars.* Toronto: John Wiley & Sons, 1999.

Loescher, Burt Garfield. *Genesis Rogers' Rangers. Volume II, The First Green Berets.* Bowie, MD: Heritage Books, Inc., 2000 (1969).

_____. *The History of Rogers Rangers. Volume I, The Beginnings, Jan. 1755–April 6, 1758*. Bowie, MD: Heritage Books, Inc., 2001, 1946.

_____. *The History of Rogers' Rangers. Volume IV, The St. Francis Raid*. Bowie, MD: Heritage Books, Inc., 2002.

MacLeod, D.P. *The Canadian Iroquois and the Seven Years' War*. Toronto: Dundurn Press, 1996.

Stanley, George F. *Canada's Soldiers, 1604–1954: The Military History of an Unmilitary People*. Toronto: Macmillan Company of Canada, 1960.

Steele, Ian K. *Betrayals: Fort William Henry and the Massacre*. New York: Oxford University Press, 1990.

Todish, Timothy J. *The Annotated and Illustrated Journals of Major Robert Rogers*. Fleischmanns, NY: Purple Mountain Press, 2002.

Warfare on the Colonial American Frontier: The Journals of Major Robert Rogers [Journals of Major Robert Rogers] & An Historical Account of the Expedition Against the Ohio Natives in the Year 1764, Under the Command of Henry Bouquet, Esq. (Reprinted from an original 1769 Edition - Bargersville, IN: Dreslar Publishing, 2001).

INDEX

Abenaki, 19–20, 29, 67, 89

Abercromby, Major-General James, 89, 100–01, 104, 116, 117, 122

Algonquins, 19, 29, 30, 102

Amherst, Major-General Jeffery, 115, 124

Battle of the Snowshoes, 100

Beauport, 129

Bougainville, Colonel, 44–5, 58, 59, 79, 109, 118, 119

Bouquet, Colonel Henry, 50–1

Braddock, Major-General Edward, 14, 60–1

Burning the North Shore, 122

Canadian way of war, 43–61, 109, 112, 121, 134

Carignan-Salières Regiment, 32, 34–5, 36, 41, 43

Champlain, Samuel de, 15, 28–30

Compagnies Franches de la Marine, 39–40, 92

coureur de bois, 21

Crown Point, 89, 115

European way of war, 53–5, 69

Fort Beausejour, 88

Fort Chambly, 83

Fort Edward, 64, 65, 83, 85, 86, 99–101, 103, 104, 107

Fort Frontenac, 14, 125

Fort Niagara, 14, 103, 124

Fort Sainte-Anne, 104

Fort St. Frédéric, 59, 83, 84, 90, 92

Fort Ticonderoga, 46, 83, 84, 88, 90, 92, 96, 98, 100, 104, 111, 113, 116, 117, 122

Fort William Henry, 11, 19, 83, 86, 88, 92, 98, 103, 116, 117, 119

Fort William Henry Massacre, 84–6, 93

Goreham's Rangers, 67–8

Huron, 27, 29, 30, 50

Iroquois, 25, 26–7, 28, 29–32, 33, 34, 35–7, 38–9, 40, 43, 50, 125

Jesuits, 15, 49–50

Johnson, Major-General William, 64, 65, 84

L'Anse-au-Foulon, 126

La Malgue, Joseph Marin de la (*see also* Marin), 96, 100–03, 105, 106, 107

la petite guerre, 46, 102, 125, 134

Lake Champlain, 11, 14, 33, 66, 83, 86, 87, 88, 90–1, 101, 109, 113, 115, 116, 117, 134

Lake George, 19, 63, 83, 84, 87–8, 91, 98, 99, 103, 111

Langlade, Charles de, 92, 93

Langy, 88–90

Louisbourg, Fortress, 14, 68, 123, 125, 127, 131–32, 134

Marin, 96, 100–03, 105, 106, 107

militia, 11, 14, 16, 34, 37, 40–1, 46, 56, 57, 58, 61, 65, 85, 119, 121, 125

Mohawk, 27, 36, 38, 67

Montcalm, Lieutenant-General Louis-Joseph Marquis de, 45, 46, 79, 85–6, 88–9, 96, 100, 109–13, 116–20, 121–30

Montgeron, Jean-Baptiste Levrault de Langis (*see also* Langy), 88–90

Montreal, 14, 44, 83, 86, 89–90, 96, 101–02, 109, 132–34

New England, 19–20, 56, 67, 131–32

New France, 14, 23, 25–30, 32–4, 36–7, 40–1, 43–9, 56, 60, 83, 84, 88, 102, 109, 111–13, 117, 118, 121–26, 131–34

Ohio Valley, 13, 61, 121

Plains of Abraham, 14, 46, 112, 123, 126, 127, 129–30

Pouchet, Captain Pierre, 51, 90

Putnam, Major Isaac, 94–6, 101, 104, 105

Quebec City, 14, 29, 46, 89, 111, 112, 120, 123 126, 131–32, 134

Richelieu Valley, 30, 33

Robert Rogers' Rules or Plan of Discipline, 72–8

Rogers' Rangers, 64, 66, 68, 79, 80, 84, 86, 105

Rogers, Major Robert, 20, 65–6, 70, 79, 86, 99, 103, 115

Royal Navy, 14, 121, 126, 132, 133

Sainte-Foy, 14

scalping, 15–6, 24, 119

Seven Years' War, 13–4, 53, 67, 121, 127

Shirley, Major-General William, 63, 65–7

Six Nations Confederacy, 27

smallpox, 85–7

St. Lawrence River, 33, 83, 90, 111, 123, 126, 127

Standing Orders of Rogers' Rangers, 80–2

Ticonderoga, Battle of, 117–18

torture, 15, 20, 22, 24, 95

Tracy, Lieutenant-General Alexandre de Prouville de, 32, 34, 105

Vaudreuil, Pierre de Rigaud de, 44–7, 53, 56, 58, 60, 109, 112–13, 115, 118–19, 124

Washington, George, 14, 27, 61, 119

Wolfe, Major-General James, 54, 60, 64, 78, 122, 126–27, 129, 133

Wood Creek, 63, 104

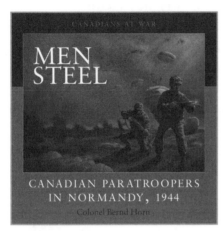

Men of Steel
Canadian Paratroopers in Normandy, 1944
Colonel Bernd Horn
978-1554887088
$19.99

Take a trip back in time to the chaos and destruction of the greatest invasion in military history, viewed through the lens of Canadian paratroopers. *Men of Steel* is the exciting story of some of Canada's toughest and most daring soldiers in the Second World War.

In the dead of night, on June 5, 1944, hundreds of elite Canadian paratroopers hurled themselves from aircraft behind enemy lines. That daring act set the stage for the eventual success of the Allied invasion fleet. From aircraft formations striking out from England on a turbulent flight across the English Channel to the tumultuous drop over Occupied Europe and deadly close combat in the Normandy countryside, *Men of Steel* is a detailed account of Canadian paratroopers and their instrumental role in D-Day.

MORE GREAT DUNDURN TITLES
FOR YOUNG ADULTS

To Stand and Fight Together
Richard Pierpoint and the Coloured Corps of Upper Canada
Steve Pitt
978-1-550027310
$19.99

In 1812, a 67-year-old black United Empire Loyalist named Richard Pierpoint helped raise "a corps of Coloured Men to stand and fight together" against the Americans who were threatening to invade the tiny British colony of Upper Canada.

Pierpoint's unique fighting unit would not only see service throughout the War of 1812, it would also be the first colonial military unit reactiviated to quash the Rebellion of 1837. It would go on to serve as a police force, keeping the peace among the competing Irish immigrant gangs during the construction of the Welland Canal.

Pierpoint and the Coloured Corps are the central focus, but the sidebars featuring fascinating facts about the rise and fall of slavery in North America and the state of African-Canadians in early Canada provide an entertaining and informative supplement. Among other tidbits, readers will find out why "Good Queen Bess" launched the British slave industry and how Scottish pineapples are connected to the American Declaration of Independence.

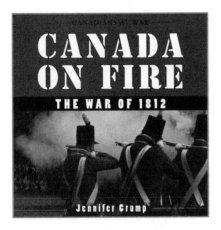

Canada on Fire
The War of 1812
Jennifer Crump
978-1554887538
$19.99

The summer of 1812 saw the beginning of one of the most brutal wars to take place on Canadian soil. With more than 1,600 people killed and a battlefront that extended from Halifax Harbour in Nova Scotia to the Columbia River in what is now British Columbia, the war featured many brave men and women who fended off much larger American forces.

Canada on Fire is an exciting account of the War of 1812 as told through the stories of the heroes who helped to defend Canada, people such as Mohawk Chief John Norton, who led a small army into battle against the wishes of his tribe, and Red George Macdonnell, who spent the war defending the St. Lawrence River.

Available at your favourite bookseller.

DUNDURN
www.dundurn.com

What did you think of this book?
Visit *www.dundurn.com* for reviews, videos, updates, and more!